READ WELL®
Plus

# The Absent Author

# Teacher's Guide

## Unit 25

Review

*Note:* See New and Important Objectives on page 2 for a complete list of skills taught and reviewed.

## Critical Foundations in Primary Reading

Marilyn Sprick, Ann Watanabe, Karen Akiyama-Paik, and Shelley V. Jones

Sopris West®
EDUCATIONAL SERVICES

A Cambium Learning® Company

BOSTON, MA • LONGMONT, CO

ISBN 13-digit: 978-1-60218-548-7
ISBN 10-digit: 1-60218-548-4

7  8  9  10  11   B&B   16  15  14  13  12

167089/6-12

# Table of Contents
## Unit 25
## The Absent Author

# Table of Contents

# Table of Contents

# Read Well 2 Sequence and Sound Pronunciation Guide

## Letter Sounds and Combinations

Cumulative Review of *Read Well 1* Sounds and Combinations (Ss, Ee, ee, Mm, Aa, Dd, th, Nn, Tt, Ww, Ii, Th, Hh, Cc, Rr, ea, sh, Sh, Kk, -ck, oo, ar, wh, Wh, ĕ, -y as in fly, Ll, Oo, Bb, all, Gg, Ff, Uu, er, oo as in book, Yy, a schwa, Pp, ay, Vv, Qq, Jj, Xx, or, Zz, a_e, -y as in baby, i_e, ou, ow as in cow, ch, Ch, ai, igh, o_e, ir) and:

| Unit 2 | Unit 3 | | Unit 5 | Unit 6 |
|---|---|---|---|---|
| **aw**<br>/aw/<br>**Paw**<br>Voiced | **ew**<br>/ōō/<br>**Crew**<br>Voiced | **ue**<br>/ōō/<br>**Blue**<br>Voiced | **u_e**<br>/ōō/<br>**Flute**<br>Bossy E Voiced | **ow**<br>/ōōō/<br>**Snow**<br>Voiced (Long) | **ge**<br>/j/<br>**Page**<br>Voiced |

| Unit 6 | Unit 7 | | Unit 8 | | Unit 10 |
|---|---|---|---|---|---|
| **-dge**<br>/j/<br>**Badge**<br>Voiced | **ci**<br>/sss/<br>**Circle**<br>Unvoiced | **ce**<br>/sss/<br>**Center**<br>Unvoiced | **kn**<br>/nnn/<br>**Knee**<br>Voiced | **ph**<br>/fff/<br>**Phone**<br>Unvoiced | **oa**<br>/ōōō/<br>**Boat**<br>Voiced (Long) |

| Unit 11 | | Unit 12 | | Unit 13 |
|---|---|---|---|---|
| **oi**<br>/oi/<br>**Point**<br>Voiced | **ea**<br>/ĕĕĕ/<br>**Bread**<br>Voiced (Short) | **gi**<br>/j/<br>**Giraffe**<br>Voiced | **au**<br>/au/<br>**Astronaut**<br>Voiced | **oy**<br>/oy/<br>**Boy**<br>Voiced |

## Affixes (including morphographs—affixes taught with meaning) and Open Syllables

Cumulative Review of *Read Well 1* Affixes (-ed, -en, -es, -ing, -ly, -s, -y, -tion) and:

| Unit 2 | Unit 3 | | Unit 5 | | Unit 6 |
|---|---|---|---|---|---|
| **re-**<br>**Means again**<br>as in reread | **un-**<br>**Means not**<br>as in unhappy | **ex-**<br>as in excited | **o**<br>Open syllable<br>/ō/<br>as in open and moment | **-ful**<br>**Means full of**<br>as in colorful | **bi-**<br>**Means two**<br>as in bicycle |

| Unit 7 | Unit 8 | Unit 11 | Unit 12 | Unit 13 | |
|---|---|---|---|---|---|
| **de-**<br>as in detective | **-able**<br>as in comfortable | **i**<br>Open syllable<br>/ī/<br>as in silence and pilot | **be-**<br>as in before | **-ous**<br>as in enormous | **dis-**<br>as in discover |

| Unit 14 | | Unit 15 | | Unit 16 | |
|---|---|---|---|---|---|
| **-al**<br>as in animal | **-ible**<br>as in flexible | **-or**<br>**Means one who**<br>as in actor | **-ment**<br>as in apartment | **-ic**<br>as in scientific | **pre-**<br>**Means before**<br>as in preview |

| Unit 17 | | Unit 18 | | Unit 19 | |
|---|---|---|---|---|---|
| **-ity**<br>as in activity | **-sion**<br>as in permission | **-ness**<br>as in fairness | **-less**<br>**Means without**<br>as in helpless | **in-**<br>as in insert | **im-**<br>**Means not**<br>as in impossible |

# Introduction
# The Absent Author

## Story Notes

***The Absent Author:*** Dink Duncan and his friends Josh and Ruth Rose are worried when mystery author Wallis Wallace fails to show up for a book signing. After all, the author had said that short of being kidnapped, nothing could stop him from coming. The intrepid trio retraces Wallis Wallace's trip to Green Lawn and solves the mystery of the absent author.

> **CAUTION**
> **(Reminder)**
> Do not read the Read Aloud recommendations during small group instruction. Reserve this time for students to read.

## Recommended Read Alouds

The *Read Well 2* suggested Read Alouds enhance small group instruction—providing opportunities to further build background knowledge and vocabulary.

### ***The Bald Bandit*** by Ron Roy

### Fiction • Mystery

The next book in the A to Z Mysteries series finds our intrepid trio hot on the trail of a videotape of a bank robbery.

### ***Read Well*** Connections
Students can test their wits trying to solve these two mysteries. They can practice identifying clues and using them to draw conclusions. Students who enjoy mysteries may want to continue on through the alphabetical series.

### NOTE FROM THE AUTHORS

> **CONGRATULATIONS TO YOU AND YOUR STUDENTS!**
> This unit is the end of *Read Well 2 Plus*. By all measures, your second grade students are reading well above grade level. They have mastered difficult biographies, learned about timelines, written summaries and reports, and appreciated fictional stories full of absurdities, suspense, and humor.
>
> Early success in reading has been shown to be a strong predictor of later success.
> You can predict with a high degree of certainty that your students will continue to do well as they move into the intermediate grades and above.

# New and Important Objectives
## A Research-Based Reading Program

## Phonics

### Cumulative Letter Sounds and Combinations

**Review** • Ss, Ee, ee, Mm, Aa, Dd, th, Nn, Tt, Ww, Ii, Th, Hh, Cc, Rr, ea, sh, Sh, Kk, -ck, oo, ar, wh, Wh, ĕ, -y (as in fly), Ll, Oo, Bb, all, Gg, Ff, Uu, er, oo (as in book), Yy, a (schwa), Pp, ay, Vv, Qq, Jj, Xx, or, Zz, a_e, -y (as in baby), i_e, ou, ow (as in cow), ch, Ch, ai, igh, o_e, ir, aw, ew, ue, u_e, ow (as in snow), ge, -dge, ci, ce, kn, ph, oa, oi, ea (as in bread), gi, au, oy

### Cumulative Affixes, Morphographs, and Open Syllables

**Review** • -ed, -en, -er, -es, -est, -ing, -ly, -s, -y, -tion, re-, un-, ex-, o (as in open), -ful, bi-, de-, -able, i (as in silence), be-, dis-, -ous, -al, -ible, -or, -ment, -ic, pre-, -ity, -sion, -ness, -less, in-, im-

### ★ New Abbreviations

Apts., Ct., E, La., N, Rd., S, W

### ★ New Contractions

ain't, how'd, o'clock, that'll, what'd, what're, who'd, why's

### ★ New Proper Nouns

Acorn Apartments, Adam's apple, Amy, Boxwood Lane, Bradley Airport, Bridge Lane, Connecticut ◆ Dink, Dink's ◆ Donald David Duncan, Eagle Lane, Eddie Carini, Ellie, Ellie's Diner, Furry Feet Pet Shop, Grampa, Green Lawn Savings Bank, Howard, Howard's ◆ Barbershop, Jimmy Fallon, Jimmy Fallon's, Jimmy's, ◆ Josh Pinto, Josh's, Lawrence Taxi, Livvy Nugent's, Livvy's, Loretta ◆ Maine, Marilyn Monroe, Maureen Higgins, Maureen's, Mavis Green, Mavis's, Moose Manor, Mr. Duncan, Mr. Linkletter ◆ Mr. Paskey, Mr. Paskey's, ◆ Mrs. Davis, Mystic Greenhouse, New England Airlines, Olivia Nugent, Pheasant La., Quail Run Road, Randy, Ron's Bait ◆ Ruth Rose, Shangri-La Hotel ◆ Squaw Island, Swan Pond, Thistle Court, Thrush Ct., Tommy Tomko ◆ Wallis Wallace, Wallis Wallace's, Woodcock Cross, Woodview Road, Woody Street, Wren Dr.

### ★ New Pattern Words

blot, blotted, bursting, cab, chat, crime, crunch, crunching, draped, firmly ◆ gee ◆ geez, ghost, haw, launch, maid, maid's, mass, nope, oozed, paused, pie, scrawled, smeared, smudge, smudged, spill, spilled, streamed, stunned, tag ◆ trots, um, urged, yanked ◆ yep ◆ yikes, yowl

**\*Known Pattern Words With Affixes** • backed, blushed, bobbed, bouncing, braces, bravely, brushing, bugging, bumping, bunches, coins, cops, dived, folding, framed, grinning, handful, hops, housing, jerked, keys, likely, louder, lunches, munches, munching, palms, patted, petting, phoned, pills, pressed, replaceable, replaced, restless, saddest, scooting, scraping, shifted, shooed, shown, shyly, sighing, smoothly, spotlessly, squinted, sweating, sweetly, teased, thrusting, trooped, tucking, twirled, unwrapped, wiping

---

\* **Known Pattern Words With Affixes, Known Tricky Words With Affixes,** and **Known Multisyllabic Words With Affixes** have base words students have previously read. The words are new in this unit because they have not been previously read with the affix.

★ = New in this unit

◆ = Words that are not introduced in the exercises before they are read in the storybook

## Phonics (continued)

### ★ New Compound and Hyphenated Words

babysitter ◆ bookshelf ◆ bookstore, bulldozer ◆ checkout, clipboard, coveralls, crossword, doorknob ◆ double-dipper, eyebrows, eyeglasses, forehead, fuddy-duddy ◆ grownups ◆ hairbrush, headache, lemonade, lunchbox, overheard ◆ raincoat, strawberry, triple-decker, workout, workouts

### ★ Other New Multisyllabic Words

absence, accomplice, adjust, adjusted ◆ apron, assume, autograph, autographed, aware, barrettes, celebrity, concentrating, conclusion, conclusions, cottage, curly, dedicate, devour, devours, dinky, drawer, driver, drivers, droopy, elderly, eon, explanation, expression ◆ fella, fitness, forgive, gesture, grassy, guilty, guinea, handkerchief, immediately, innocently, interrupt, interrupted, interruption, investigate, itinerary, jiggle, jiggling, kennel, ketchup, kiddie, kidding, lobby, loopy, loyal, madam, mayonnaise, mentally, mercy, muffled, mustard, napkin, napkins, nutty, pardon, peckish, phantom, pharmacy, pillow, preserve, previous, public, raisin, ransom, rational, reflected, relieved, rental, reserve, revolving, riddle, satisfied, scribbled, signature, signatures ◆ sneakers, spooky, stroller, stupidly, suspicious, tennis, timid, timidly, triple, tuna, veterinarian, victim, vividly

*Known Multisyllabic Words With Affixes • approached, arrangements, arrives, communicates, disturbed, foolishness, gardening ◆ gotta, handling, kidnapper ◆ kinda, lobsters ◆ lotta, mommy's, nervously, orders, poisoned, practically, prepared, reopened, rummaged, suggesting, swallowing, telephoned, trembly, wobbled, writers, yesterday's

### ★ New Tricky Words

cough, coughing, courts, gym, mischievous, mustache, peculiar, pistachio, scheme, senior

*Known Tricky Words With Affixes • answering, earlier, guys, merriest, mysteries, mysterious, signing, thoughtfully, thoughts, untie, untied ◆ woulda

## Fluency

Accuracy, Expression, Phrasing, Rate

## Vocabulary

**New** • accomplice, adjust, arrangement, assume, celebrity, dedicate, definitely, devour, disturb, gesture, innocently, itinerary, mischievous, muffled, mystery peculiar, prefer, preserve, previous, relieved, restless, satisfied, stunned, suspect, suspicion, suspicious, vividly

**Review** • common, congratulate, dangerous, determined, disappointed, disguise, distressed, fascinating, habit, honor, imitate, impressed, inspiration, mention, mood, opinion, perfect, pretend, recognize, responsible, retrace, review, suspect, suspense

**Reviewed in Context** • accidentally, advice, advisor, brilliant, cause, communicate, concerned, confused, definitely, disappointed, disguise, except, expect, imagination, imitate, impressed, liquid, mention, mystery, offer, opinion, original, owe, peer, perfect, perhaps, pretend, recognize, responsible, review, scurry, suspect, swamp, unless, upset, volume, wealthy wonderful

### Idioms and Expressions

**New** • cat's out of the bag, smells fishy, tied up

# Comprehension

**Unit Genres**

**Fiction** • Mystery

**Comprehension Processes**

Build Knowledge: Factual, Procedural, Conceptual

| Day | 1 | 2 | 3 | 4 | 5 | 6 | 7 | 8 | 9 |
|---|---|---|---|---|---|---|---|---|---|
| **Remember** | | | | | | | | | |
| Defining | | | | | | | | | |
| Identifying (recalling) | S,C | S,C | S,C | S | C | S,C | S,C | S,C | |
| Using | | | | S | | | | | |
| **Understand** | | | | | | | | | |
| Defining (in your own words) | S | S,C | C | | S | | S | S | |
| Describing | S | S | S,C | S | | | | | |
| Explaining (rephrasing) | S,C | S,C | S | S | S | C | S,C | S | |
| Illustrating | C | C | | | | | | | |
| Sequencing | | C | | | | | | | |
| Summarizing | C | S,C | S,C | S,C | S,C | S,C | S,C | S,C | |
| Using | S | S,C | S,C | S | S | S | S | S,C | S |
| Visualizing | | | | | | | | | |
| **Apply** | | | | | | | | | |
| Demonstrating | | S | | | | | | | |
| Explaining (unstated) | S | S,C | S | S | S | | S,C | S | S |
| Illustrating | | | | | | | | | |
| Inferring | S,C | S,C | S,C | S | S | S | S | S | S |
| Making Connections (relating) | S | | | | | | S | | |
| Predicting | S | S | S | S | S | S | S | | S |
| Using | S | S | S | S | S | S,C | S,C | S | S |
| **Analyze** | | | | | | | | | |
| Classifying | S | S | | | | | | S | |
| Comparing/Contrasting | | S,C | S | | | | | | |
| Distinguishing Cause/Effect | | | | | | | | | |
| Drawing Conclusions | S | S,C | S | S,C | S,C | S,C | S,C | S | S |
| Inferring | S | | | | | | | | |
| **Evaluate** | | | | | | | | | |
| Making Judgments | | | | | | | | | S |
| Responding (personal) | | | | S | | C | C | S,C | |
| **Create** | | | | | | | | | |
| Generating Ideas | S,C | S | S,C | C | | S | C | | |

E = Exercise, S = Storybook, C = Comprehension & Skill

4

# Comprehension (continued)

## Skills and Strategies

| Day | 1 | 2 | 3 | 4 | 5 | 6 | 7 | 8 | 9 |
|---|---|---|---|---|---|---|---|---|---|
| **Priming Background Knowledge** | | | | | | | | | |
| **Setting a Purpose for Reading** | | S | S | S | S | S | S | S | |
| **Answering Questions** | S,C | S | S | S | S | S | S | S | S |
| **Asking Questions** | C | | S,C | | | | | | |
| **Visualizing** | | | | | | | | | |
| **Comprehension Monitoring/Fix Ups** | | | | | | | | | |
| Does it Make Sense? | | C | | | C | | | | |
| Looking Back | | | | | | | | | |
| Restating | | | | | | | | | |
| **Summarizing** | | | | | | | | | |
| Main Idea | | | | | | | | | |
| Retelling | | | | | | | | | |
| Supporting Details | | | | | | | | | |
| **Understanding Text Structure** | | | | | | | | | |
| Title, Author, Illustrator | S | | | | | | | | |
| Fact or Fiction | | | | | | | | | |
| Genre (Classifying) | | | | | | | | | |
| **Narrative** | | | | | | | | | |
| Setting | S | | | | | | | | |
| Main Character/Traits (Characterization) | S,C | | | S | | C | | | |
| Goal | | | | | | | | | |
| Problem/Solution | S,C | S | | | | | | S | |
| Action/Events/Sequence | | C | S | | | | | | |
| Outcome/Conclusion | | | | | | | | | |
| Lesson/Author's Message | | | | | | | | | |
| **Expository** | | | | | | | | | |
| Subject/Topic | | | | | | | | | |
| Heading | | | | | | | | | |
| Supporting Details (Facts/Information) | | | | | | | C | | |
| Main Idea | | | | | | | | | |
| **Using Graphic Organizers** | | | | | | | | | |
| Chart | | | | | | | | | |
| Diagram (labeling) | | | | | | | | | |
| Hierarchy (topic/detail) | | | | | | | C | | |
| K-W-L | | | | | | | | | |
| Map (locating, labeling) | S | | S | S,C | | | | | |
| Matrix (compare/contrast) | | | | | | | | | |
| Sequence (linear, cycle, cause and effect) | | | | | | | | | |
| Story Map | | | | | | | | | |
| Web | | | | | | | | | |

E = Exercise, S = Storybook, C = Comprehension & Skill

# Comprehension (continued)

## Study Skills

| Day | 1 | 2 | 3 | 4 | 5 | 6 | 7 | 8 | 9 |
|---|---|---|---|---|---|---|---|---|---|
| Alphabetical Order | | | | C | | | | | |
| Following Directions | | | | | C | | | | |
| Locating Information | | | | | | | | | |
| Note Taking | C | C | C | C | C | C | C | C | |
| Previewing | | | | | | | | | |
| Reviewing | | S | S | S | S | S | S | S | S |
| Test Taking | | C | | | | | | | |
| Using Glossary | | | | | | | | | |
| Using Table of Contents | | | | | | | | | |
| Viewing | S | | | | | C | C | C | |
| Verifying | | | | | | | | | |

## Writing in Response to Reading

| Day | 1 | 2 | 3 | 4 | 5 | 6 | 7 | 8 | 9 |
|---|---|---|---|---|---|---|---|---|---|
| Sentence Completion | C | C | C | C | C | C | C | C | |
| Making Lists | | | | | | | | | |
| Sentence Writing | C | | | | | | C | | |
| Story Retell/Summary | | | | | | | | | |
| Fact Summary | | | | | | | | | |
| Paragraph Writing | C | | | | | | C | | |
| Report Writing | | | | | | | | | |
| Open-Ended Response | | | | | | C | C | | |
| Creative Writing | | | | | | C | | | |

## Writing Traits

(Addressed within the context of Writing in Response to Reading)

| Day | 1 | 2 | 3 | 4 | 5 | 6 | 7 | 8 | 9 |
|---|---|---|---|---|---|---|---|---|---|
| **Ideas and Content** | | | | | | | | | |
| Elaborating/Generating | | | | | | | C | | |
| **Organization** | | | | | | | | | |
| Introduction | | | | | | | | | |
| Topic Sentence | | | | | | | C | | |
| Supporting Details | | | | | | | C | | |
| Sequencing | | | | | | | | | |
| **Word Choice** | | | | | | | | | |
| Sophisticated Words (Tier 2 and 3) | C | | | | | | C | | |
| **Conventions** | | | | | | | | | |
| Capital | C | | C | C | C | C | C | C | |
| Ending Punctuation | C | C | C | C | C | C | C | | |
| Other (commas, quotation marks) | | | | | | | | | |
| **Presentation** | | | | | | | | | |
| Handwriting | C | | | | | | C | | |
| Neatness | C | | | | | | C | | |

E = Exercise, S = Storybook, C = Comprehension & Skill

# Daily Lesson Planning

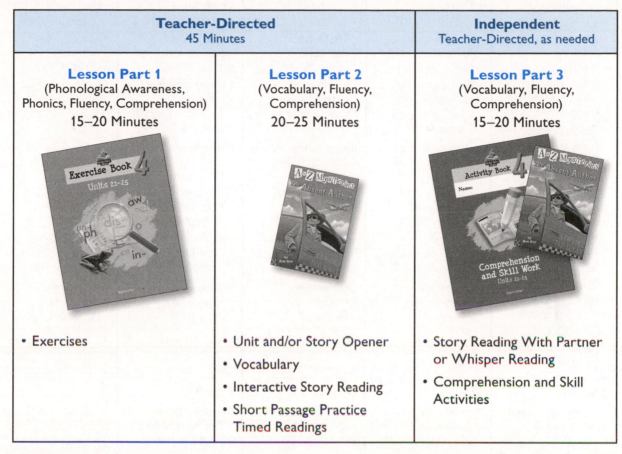

| Teacher-Directed 45 Minutes | | Independent Teacher-Directed, as needed |
|---|---|---|
| **Lesson Part 1** (Phonological Awareness, Phonics, Fluency, Comprehension) 15–20 Minutes | **Lesson Part 2** (Vocabulary, Fluency, Comprehension) 20–25 Minutes | **Lesson Part 3** (Vocabulary, Fluency, Comprehension) 15–20 Minutes |
| • Exercises | • Unit and/or Story Opener<br>• Vocabulary<br>• Interactive Story Reading<br>• Short Passage Practice Timed Readings | • Story Reading With Partner or Whisper Reading<br>• Comprehension and Skill Activities |

## HOMEWORK

*Read Well* Homework (blackline masters of new *Read Well 2* passages) provides an opportunity for children to celebrate accomplishments with parents. Homework should be sent home on routine days.

## ORAL READING FLUENCY ASSESSMENT

Upon completion of this unit, assess each student.

| **Day 1** | **Day 2** | **Day 3** | **Day 4** | **Day 5** |
|---|---|---|---|---|
| **Teacher-Directed**<br>• Exercise 1<br>• Story Opener: The Absent Author<br>• Vocabulary, Ch. 1, 2<br>• Absent Author, Ch. 1<br>• Guide practice: Case Log Entry 1a, 1b, Comp & Skill 1<br><br>**Independent Work**<br>• On Your Own: Partner or Whisper Read, The Absent Author, Ch. 2<br>• Case Log Entries 1a, 1b, Comp & Skill 1<br><br>**Homework**<br>• Homework Passage 1 | **Teacher-Directed**<br>• Exercise 2<br>• Vocabulary, Ch. 3<br>• The Absent Author, Ch. 3, pages 18–23<br>• Guide practice, as needed, on Case Log Entry 2, Comp & Skill 2<br><br>**Independent Work**<br>• On Your Own: Partner or Whisper Read, The Absent Author, Ch. 3, pages 24–27<br>• Case Log Entry 2, Comp & Skill 2<br><br>**Homework**<br>• Homework Passage 2 | **Teacher-Directed**<br>• Exercise 3<br>• Vocabulary, Ch. 4<br>• The Absent Author, Ch. 4, pages 28–34<br>• Guide practice, as needed, on Case Log Entry 3, Comp & Skill 3<br><br>**Independent Work**<br>• On Your Own: Partner or Whisper Read, The Absent Author, Ch. 4, pages 34–39<br>• Case Log Entry 3, Comp & Skill 3<br><br>**Homework**<br>• Homework Passage 3 | **Teacher-Directed**<br>• Exercise 4<br>• Vocabulary, Ch. 5<br>• The Absent Author, Ch. 5, pages 40–42<br>• Guide practice, as needed, on Case Log Entry 4, Comp & Skill 4<br><br>**Independent Work**<br>• On Your Own: Partner or Whisper Read, The Absent Author, Ch. 5, pages 43–46<br>• Case Log Entry 4, Comp & Skill 4<br><br>**Homework**<br>• Homework Passage 4 | **Teacher-Directed**<br>• Exercise 5<br>• Vocabulary, Ch. 6<br>• The Absent Author, Ch. 6, pages 47–50<br>• Guide practice, as needed, on Comp & Skill 5, Case Log Entry 5<br><br>**Independent Work**<br>• On Your Own: Partner or Whisper Read, The Absent Author, Ch. 6, pages 51–55<br>• Case Log Entry 5, Comp & Skill 5<br><br>**Homework**<br>• Homework Passage 5 |

| **Day 6** | **Day 7** | **Day 8** | **Day 9** | |
|---|---|---|---|---|
| **Teacher-Directed**<br>• Exercise 6<br>• Vocabulary, Ch. 7<br>• The Absent Author, Ch. 7, pages 56–60<br>• Guide practice, as needed, on Case Log Entry 6, Comp & Skill 6a and 6b<br><br>**Independent Work**<br>• On Your Own: Partner or Whisper Read, The Absent Author, Ch. 7, pages 61–65<br>• Case Log Entry 6, Comp & Skill 6a and 6b<br><br>**Homework**<br>• Homework Passage 6 | **Teacher-Directed**<br>• Exercise 7<br>• Vocabulary, Ch. 8, 9<br>• The Absent Author, Ch. 8<br>• Guide practice, as needed, on Case Log Entry 7, Comp & Skill 7a and 7b<br><br>**Independent Work**<br>• On Your Own: Partner or Whisper Read, The Absent Author, Ch. 9<br>• Case Log Entry 7, Comp & Skill 7a and 7b<br><br>**Homework**<br>• Homework Passage 7 | **Teacher-Directed**<br>• Exercise 8<br>• Vocabulary, Ch. 10<br>• The Absent Author, Ch. 10, pages 76–81<br>• Guide practice: Case Log Entry 8, Comp & Skill 8a and 8b<br><br>**Independent Work**<br>• On Your Own: Partner or Whisper Read, The Absent Author, Ch. 10, pages 82–87<br>• Case Log Entry 8, Comp & Skill 8a and 8b<br><br>**Homework**<br>• Homework Passage 8 | **Teacher-Directed**<br>• The Annual Read Well Literary Awards (Closing Ceremonies)<br>• Oral Reading Fluency Assessment*<br><br>**Independent Work**<br>• Just for Fun (optional)<br><br>**Homework**<br>• Homework Passage 9 | |

*Note:* Unit 25 features an extra Just for Fun Comp & Skill activity, located after Activity 8b. This page can be used as independent work on Day 9 or at any time during the unit.

*The Oral Reading Fluency Assessments are individually administered by the teacher. Start giving Oral Reading Fluency Assessments on Day 7 while students are working on their Comprehension and Skill Activities.

# Materials and Materials Preparation

## Core Lessons

### Teacher Materials

**READ WELL 2 MATERIALS**

- Unit 25 Teacher's Guide
- Sound Cards
- Unit 25 Oral Reading Fluency Assessment on page 143
- Group Assessment Record found in the *Assessment Manual*

**SCHOOL SUPPLIES**

Stopwatch or watch with a second hand

### Student Materials

**READ WELL 2 MATERIALS (for each student)**

- *The Absent Author*
- *Exercise Book 4*
- *Activity Book 4* or copies of Unit 25 Comprehension and Skill Work
- Unit 25 Certificate of Achievement (BLM, page 144)
- Unit 25 Homework (blackline masters)
  See *Getting Started* for suggested homework routines.

**SCHOOL SUPPLIES**

Pencils, colors (optional—markers, crayons, or colored pencils)

Make one copy per student of each blackline master, as appropriate for the group.

*Note:* For new or difficult Comprehension and Skill Activities, make overhead transparencies from the blackline masters. Use the transparencies to demonstrate and guide practice.

**SPECIAL NOTE**

Your students will complete a Case Log in this unit. For ease of use, pull pages 71–80 from *Activity Book 4*. Staple the pages together into a book.

# How to Teach the Lessons

Teach from this section. Each instructional component is outlined in an easy-to-teach format.

## Exercise 1

- Story Opener: The Absent Author
- Vocabulary
- Story Reading 1
  With the Teacher: Chapter 1
  On Your Own: Chapter 2
- Case Log Entries 1a and 1b, Comprehension and Skill Activity 1

## Exercise 2

- Vocabulary
- Story Reading 2
  With the Teacher: Chapter 3, Pages 18–23
  On Your Own: Chapter 3, Pages 24–27
- Case Log Entry 2, Comprehension and Skill Activity 2

## Exercise 3

- Vocabulary
- Story Reading 3
  With the Teacher: Chapter 4, Pages 28–34
  On Your Own: Chapter 4, Pages 34–39
- Case Log Entry 3, Comprehension and Skill Activity 3

## Exercise 4

- Vocabulary
- Story Reading 4
  With the Teacher: Chapter 5, Pages 40–42
  On Your Own: Chapter 5, Pages 43–46
- Case Log Entry 4, Comprehension and Skill Activity 4

## Exercise 5

- Vocabulary
- Story Reading 5
  With the Teacher: Chapter 6, Pages 47–50
  On Your Own: Chapter 6, Pages 51–55
- Case Log Entry 5, Comprehension and Skill Activity 5

*Note:* Lessons include daily homework.

## Exercise 6

- Vocabulary
- Story Reading 6
  With the Teacher: Chapter 7, Pages 56–60
  On Your Own: Chapter 7, Pages 61–65
- Case Log Entry 6, Comprehension and Skill
  Activities 6a and 6b

## Exercise 7

- Vocabulary
- Story Reading 7
  With the Teacher: Chapter 8
  On Your Own: Chapter 9
- Case Log Entry 7, Comprehension and Skill
  Activities 7a and 7b

## Exercise 8

- Vocabulary
- Story Reading 8
  With the Teacher: Chapter 10, Pages 76–81
  On Your Own: Chapter 10, Pages 82–87
- Case Log Entry 8, Comprehension and Skill
  Activities 8a and 8b

## Story Reading 9

With the Teacher: The Annual *Read Well* Literary
Awards (Closing Ceremonies)
(Optional) Comprehension and Skill Activity,
Just for Fun: *Read Well* Literary Awards

*Note:* Lessons include daily homework.

## ❶ SOUND PRACTICE

**PACING**

Exercise 1 should take about 15 minutes.

- For each task, have students spell and say the focus sound in the gray bar.
- Next, have students read each underlined sound, the word, then the whole column.
- Repeat with each column, building accuracy first, then fluency.

## ❷ ACCURACY AND FLUENCY BUILDING

- For each task, have students say any underlined part, then read the word.
- Set a pace. Then have students read the whole words in each task and column.
- Provide repeated practice, building accuracy first, then fluency.

### C1. Multisyllabic Words

- For the list of words divided by syllables, have students read each syllable, then the whole word. Use the word in a sentence, as appropriate.
- For the list of whole words, build accuracy and then fluency.

| | |
|---|---|
| **coveralls** | Dad needed to work on the car, so he put on his . . . *coveralls.* |
| **concentrating** | Cecilia was very tired and had a hard time . . . *concentrating.* |
| **mentally** | The puzzle was extremely hard. It was . . . *mentally* . . . exhausting. |
| **elderly** | My grandparents are very old. They are . . . *elderly.* |
| **kennel** | When we went on vacation, we put our dogs in a . . . *kennel.* |
| **arrangements** | Jerry had a travel agent make all the travel . . . *arrangements.* |
| **guinea** | Our class has a pet . . . *guinea* . . . pig. |
| **veterinarian** | Jodie loves animals. When she grows up, she wants to be a . . . *veterinarian.* |

### D1. Tricky Words

- For each Tricky Word, have students use the sounds and word parts they know to silently sound out the word. Use the word in a sentence to help with pronunciation.
- If the word is unfamiliar, tell students the word.

**mischievous**

Look at the first word. Say the word parts silently. Thumbs up when you know the word. Use my sentence to help you pronounce the word. Our cat is always getting into trouble. He is . . . *mischievous.* Read the word three times. (mischievous, mischievous, mischievous)

**mystic**

Look at the next word. Say the word parts silently. Thumbs up when you know the word. Use my sentence to help you pronounce the word. Something that is mysterious is . . . *mystic.* Read the word two times. (mystic, mystic)

| | |
|---|---|
| **thistle** | That prickly plant with a purple flower is a . . . *thistle.* |
| **swan** | The ugly duckling turned into a beautiful . . . *swan.* |
| **mystery** | I want to be a detective like Sir Winston and solve a . . . *mystery.* |
| **mysteries** | Detectives often solve . . . *mysteries.* |

- Have students go back and read the whole words in the column.

## ❸ WORD ENDINGS

## ❹ NAMES AND PLACES

## ❺ MORPHOGRAPHS AND AFFIXES

⑥ **GENERALIZATION: READING NEW WORDS IN PARAGRAPHS**

- Have students read the paragraph silently, then out loud. Tell students to use the sounds and word parts they know to read any difficult words.
- Repeat practice, as needed.

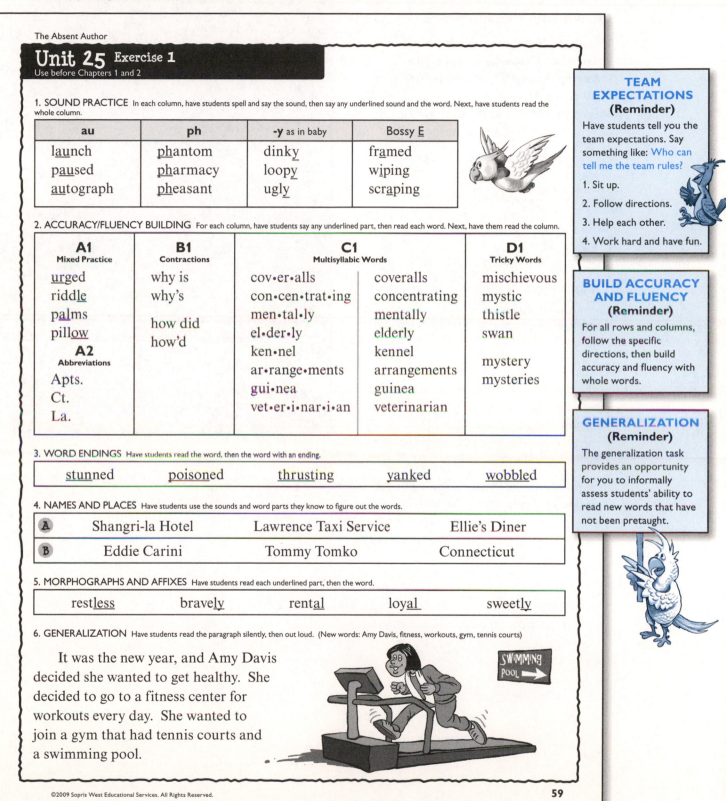

The Absent Author

## Unit 25 Exercise 1
Use before Chapters 1 and 2

**1. SOUND PRACTICE** In each column, have students spell and say the sound, then say any underlined sound and the word. Next, have students read the whole column.

| au | ph | -y as in baby | Bossy E |
|---|---|---|---|
| l<u>au</u>nch | <u>ph</u>antom | dink<u>y</u> | fram<u>e</u>d |
| p<u>au</u>sed | <u>ph</u>armacy | loop<u>y</u> | wip<u>i</u>ng |
| <u>au</u>tograph | <u>ph</u>easant | ugl<u>y</u> | scrap<u>i</u>ng |

**2. ACCURACY/FLUENCY BUILDING** For each column, have students say any underlined part, then read each word. Next, have them read the column.

| A1 Mixed Practice | B1 Contractions | C1 Multisyllabic Words | | D1 Tricky Words |
|---|---|---|---|---|
| <u>ur</u>ged | why is | cov•er•alls | coveralls | mischievous |
| ridd<u>le</u> | why's | con•cen•trat•ing | concentrating | mystic |
| p<u>al</u>ms | | men•tal•ly | mentally | thistle |
| pill<u>ow</u> | how did | el•der•ly | elderly | swan |
| **A2** Abbreviations | how'd | ken•nel | kennel | |
| Apts. | | ar•range•ments | arrangements | mystery |
| Ct. | | gui•nea | guinea | mysteries |
| La. | | vet•er•i•nar•i•an | veterinarian | |

**3. WORD ENDINGS** Have students read the word, then the word with an ending.

| stunned | poisoned | thrusting | yanked | wobbled |
|---|---|---|---|---|

**4. NAMES AND PLACES** Have students use the sounds and word parts they know to figure out the words.

| Ⓐ | Shangri-la Hotel | Lawrence Taxi Service | Ellie's Diner |
|---|---|---|---|
| Ⓑ | Eddie Carini | Tommy Tomko | Connecticut |

**5. MORPHOGRAPHS AND AFFIXES** Have students read each underlined part, then the word.

| rest<u>less</u> | brave<u>ly</u> | rent<u>al</u> | loy<u>al</u> | sweet<u>ly</u> |
|---|---|---|---|---|

**6. GENERALIZATION** Have students read the paragraph silently, then out loud. (New words: Amy Davis, fitness, workouts, gym, tennis courts)

It was the new year, and Amy Davis decided she wanted to get healthy. She decided to go to a fitness center for workouts every day. She wanted to join a gym that had tennis courts and a swimming pool.

SWIMMING POOL →

59

### TEAM EXPECTATIONS (Reminder)

Have students tell you the team expectations. Say something like: Who can tell me the team rules?

1. Sit up.
2. Follow directions.
3. Help each other.
4. Work hard and have fun.

### BUILD ACCURACY AND FLUENCY (Reminder)

For all rows and columns, follow the specific directions, then build accuracy and fluency with whole words.

### GENERALIZATION (Reminder)

The generalization task provides an opportunity for you to informally assess students' ability to read new words that have not been pretaught.

## COMPREHENSION PROCESSES

Remember, Understand, Apply, Analyze

## PROCEDURES

1. **Introducing the Storybook**

   **Viewing; Identifying—Title, Author, Illustrator; Drawing Conclusions; Inferring; Using Vocabulary—mystery; Predicting; Defining**

   Have students identify the title of their new storybook. Say something like:

   Look at the cover. What's the title of the book? (The Absent Author)

   Who's the author? (Ron Roy)

   Now turn to the title page. Who is the illustrator?
   (John Steven Gurney)

   *The Absent Author* is the first book in a series called the A to Z Mysteries. Can you guess how many books are in this series? (26)

   That's right. There's a book for each letter in the alphabet! If the first book is called *The Absent Author*, what do you think the second book might be called?
   (The Bald Bandit, The Bad Bully, The Bossy Baker . . . )

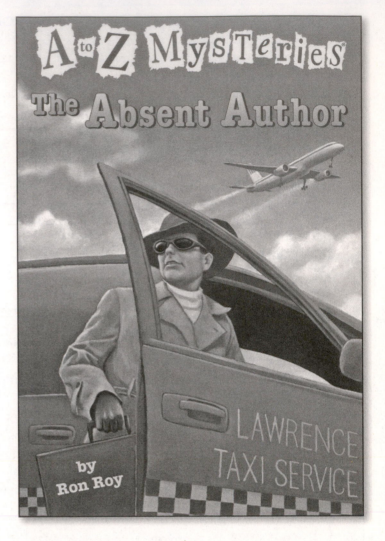

In a mystery, there's a problem, clues to follow, and a conclusion, or solution. The title of the book is *The Absent Author*.
What do you think the problem will be?
(It will be about an author who is absent.)

What does it mean to be absent? (It means that you are sick and don't go to school.)
Yes, but you can be absent from any place for any reason.
So from the title, what do we know about the author?
(He or she is absent from something. The author doesn't show up for something.)

## 2. Using the Map of Green Lawn

### Using Graphic Organizer; Identifying—Setting

Have students look at the map of Green Lawn on the two pages after the title page. Say something like:

Turn to the next pages. This book is great. It has a map of the town where the story takes place. Can you find the name of the town?

(Green Lawn)

We can use the map to keep track of where the main characters are during the story.

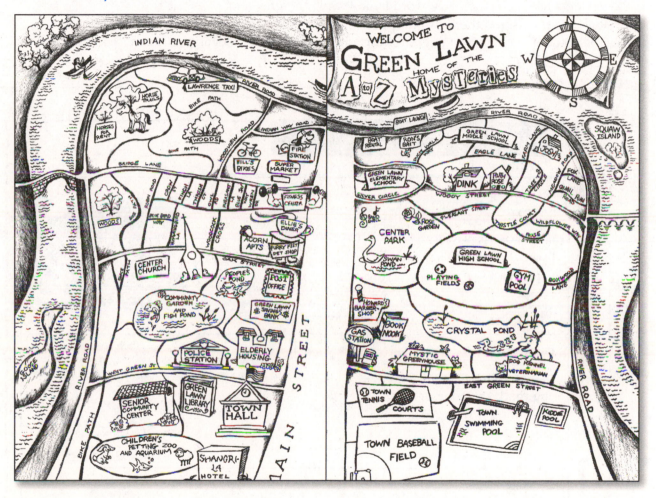

## COMPREHENSION PROCESSES

Understand, Apply

## PROCEDURES

**Introducing Vocabulary**

★mischievous, impressed ★arrangement ★restless ★stunned

- For each vocabulary word, have students read the word by parts, then read the whole word.
- Read the student-friendly explanations to students as they follow with their fingers. Then have students use the vocabulary word by following the gray text.
- Review and discuss the illustrations.

  *Note*: Student vocabulary pages for this unit are found in the students' *Exercise Book 4*.

**USING VOCABULARY**

The Absent Author

# Unit 25 Vocabulary 1
Use after Exercise 1

| ★mis·chie·vous<br><br>Someone who is **mischievous** is playful and likes to have fun. They like to play tricks on others. | The *mischievous* squirrel kept throwing nuts at us from the tree.<br><br>What's a way of describing the playful little boy who rang my doorbell, then hid in the bushes?**1**<br><br>The word *mischievous* describes the boy. What kind of word is mischievous? Mischievous is an …**2** |
| im·pressed<br><br>**Impressed** means that you think someone or something is very good. | Judy Moody was *impressed* with the poster Ben made.<br><br>What did Judy think of Ben's poster?**3** |
| ★ar·range·ment<br><br>**Arrangements** are plans or things you do so something can happen. | Mom called the vet and made *arrangements* to have them take care of our puppy while we were gone.<br><br>What did Mom do?**4** |

**❶ Apply:** Using Vocabulary—mischievous  (The little boy was mischievous.)

**❷ Analyze:** Classifying; **Apply:** Using Vocabulary—mischievous  (adjective)

**❸ Understand:** Using Vocabulary—impressed  (Judy thought Ben's poster was very good.)

**❹ Apply:** Using Vocabulary—arrangement  (Mom made plans for the vet to take care of our puppy while we were gone.  Mom made arrangements.)

★ = New in this unit

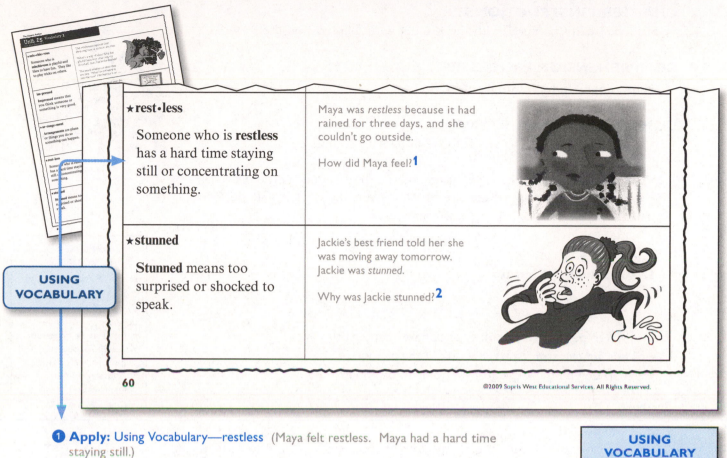

**★rest•less**

Someone who is **restless** has a hard time staying still or concentrating on something.

Maya was *restless* because it had rained for three days, and she couldn't go outside.

How did Maya feel?**1**

**★stunned**

**Stunned** means too surprised or shocked to speak.

Jackie's best friend told her she was moving away tomorrow. Jackie was *stunned*.

Why was Jackie stunned?**2**

60

❶ **Apply:** Using Vocabulary—restless (Maya felt restless. Maya had a hard time staying still.)

❷ **Apply:** Using Vocabulary—stunned (Jackie was stunned because her best friend was moving the next day. She was surprised.)

**USING VOCABULARY**

Be enthusiastic about learning new words. Keep a running list of words you would like to use and encourage students to use. Keep the list handy when you are teaching. Put students' names on the board to acknowledge use of a word. Say things like:

Wow! [Ralph] used the word *mischievous* when he told us about his little brother who ate all the cookies from the cookie jar. That's a great way to use a vocabulary word!

## CHAPTER 1 INSTRUCTIONS
Students read Chapter 1 with the teacher and Chapter 2 on their own.

## COMPREHENSION PROCESSES
**Remember, Understand, Apply, Create**

## COMPREHENSION BUILDING
- Encourage students to answer questions with complete sentences, when appropriate.
- If students have difficulty comprehending, think aloud with them or reread the portion of the story that answers the question. Repeat the question.

## PROCEDURES

**1. Introducing Chapter 1**

**Viewing, Predicting**
Say something like:

Turn to page 1. This book doesn't have chapter titles.
Let's get the story started. Look at the picture.
Who do you think the story is going to be about?

(It's going to be about two boys, about our age.)

**2. First Reading**
- Ask questions and discuss the text as indicated by the blue text in this guide.
- Mix group and individual turns, independent of your voice.
  Have students work toward a group accuracy goal of 0–6 errors.
  Quietly keep track of errors made by all students in the group.
- After reading the story, practice any difficult words.
  Repeat, if students have not reached the accuracy goal.

**3. Second Reading, Short Passage Practice: Developing Prosody**
- Demonstrate expressive, fluent reading of the first two paragraphs. Read at a rate slightly faster than the students' rate.
- Guide practice with your voice.
- Provide individual turns while others track with their fingers and whisper read.
- Repeat with one paragraph at a time.

> **REPEATED READINGS**
> **Prosody**
> On the second reading, students practice developing prosody— phrasing and expression. Research has shown that prosody is related to both fluency and comprehension.

## Chapter 1

"Please, Josh," Dink said. "If you come with me today, I'll owe you one. Just name it. *Anything!*"

Dink's full name was Donald David Duncan. But no one in Green Lawn ever called him that. Except his mother, when she meant business.

Josh Pinto grinned at his best friend.

1

2

"Anything?" He raised his mischievous green eyes toward the ceiling of Dink's bedroom. "Let's see, what do you have that I want?" He scratched his head. "I know, I'll take Loretta!"

Dink tossed a pillow at Josh. "When I said *anything*, I meant anything but my guinea pig! Are you coming with me or not? I have to be at the Book Nook in fifteen minutes!"

Dink rushed into the bathroom, tucking his shirt into his jeans at the same time. Josh followed him.

Standing in front of the mirror, Dink yanked a brush through his thick blond hair. "Well?" he asked. "Are you coming with me?"

"What's so important about this writer guy?" Josh asked, sitting on the edge of the bathtub.

Dink turned around and pointed his hairbrush. "Wallis Wallace isn't just

some writer guy, Josh. He's the most famous mystery writer in the world! All the kids read his books. Except for you."

"If he's so famous, why's he coming to dinky little Green Lawn?"

Dink charged back into his bedroom. "I told you! He's coming because I *invited* him. I'm scared to death to meet someone so famous. I don't even know what you're supposed to say to an author!"

Dink dived under his bed and backed out again with his sneakers. "Please come with me?"

Josh leaned in the bedroom doorway. "Sure I'll come, you dope. I'm just trying to make you sweat. Usually you're so calm!"

Dink stared at his friend. "You will? Thanks! I can't believe Wallis Wallace is really coming. When I wrote and asked

## After Reading Page 2

❶ **Apply:** Inferring—Character Traits (Characterization); **Understand:** Defining and Using Vocabulary—mischievous
One of the characters is Dink, and the other is Josh. We learned that Josh is mischievous. What does that mean?
(He likes to play tricks.  He is a lot of fun. He likes to make mischief.)

## After Reading Page 3

❶ **Understand:** Explaining
Why is Wallis Wallace coming to Green Lawn?
(He is coming to Green Lawn because Dink invited him.)

❷ **Understand:** Explaining
Why is Dink "scared to death"?
(He is nervous about meeting someone famous. He invited the author and doesn't know what he will say when he meets him.)

❸ **Apply:** Making Connections; **Create:** Generating Ideas
Would you be nervous if you were about to meet someone famous? What would you say to your favorite author?
(I would be excited.  I would ask how he comes up with so many ideas for stories . . . )

4

him, I never thought he'd say yes."

Dink yanked his backpack out of his closet. "Pack my books, okay? I'm getting Wallis Wallace to sign them all!"

Josh began pulling Wallis Wallace books off Dink's bookshelf. "Geez, how many do you have?"

"Every one he's written." Dink sat on the floor to tie his sneakers. "Twenty-three so far. You should read some of them, Josh."

Josh picked out *The Poisoned Pond* and read the back cover. "Hey, cool! It says here that Wallis Wallace lives in a castle in Maine! Wouldn't that be neat?"

Dink grinned. "When I'm a famous writer, you can live in my castle, Josh."

"No way. When I'm a famous *artist*, you can live in *my* castle. Down in the basement!"

Josh picked up *The Riddle in the River.* "What's this guy look like?" he

asked. "And how come his picture isn't on any of these books?"

"I wondered about that, too," Dink said. "I sent him one of my school pictures and asked for one of him. But when I got his letter, there was no picture."

He finished tying his laces. "Maybe Wallis Wallace just doesn't like having his picture taken."

Josh squeezed all twenty-three books into Dink's pack. He grinned at Dink. "Or maybe he's just too ugly."

Dink laughed. "Gee, Josh, *you're* ugly and you love having your picture taken."

"Haw, haw." Josh picked up his drawing pad. "But just because you're my best friend, I'll draw his picture at the bookstore."

Dink looked at his watch. "Yikes!" he said. "We have to pick up Ruth Rose

## After Reading Pages 4 and 5

**❶ Understand:** Describing—Character Traits (Characterization)
**What have you learned about Wallis Wallace?**
(He is a famous author. He lives in a castle in Maine. He's written 23 books. He must not like to get his picture taken. He didn't send Dink a picture, and he doesn't have his picture on his books . . . )

**❷ Understand:** Describing—Character Traits (Characterization); **Apply:** Inferring
**What have you learned so far about Dink?**
(He has blond hair. His real name is Donald David Duncan. He likes to read mysteries. He has a pet guinea pig. He wants to be an author. Dink and Josh are best friends . . . )

6

in one minute!" He tore into the bathroom and started brushing his teeth.

"How'd you get her to come?" Josh called.

Dink rushed back into his room, wiping toothpaste from his mouth. "You kidding? Ruth Rose loves Wallis Wallace's books."

Dink slung his backpack over his shoulder. He and Josh hurried next door to 24 Woody Street. Tiger, Ruth Rose's orange cat, was sitting in the sun on the steps.

Dink pressed the doorbell.

Ruth Rose showed up at the door.

As usual, she was dressed all in one color. Today it was purple. She wore purple coveralls over a purple shirt and had on purple running shoes. A purple baseball cap kept her black curls out of her face.

"Hey," she said. Then she turned

**After Reading Pages 6 and 7**

**❶ Understand:** Defining; Using Vocabulary—habit
The book says, "As usual, [Ruth Rose] was dressed all in one color." What does *as usual* mean?
(It means she always wore one color. It was her habit . . . )

**❷ Apply:** Viewing; Inferring; Using Vocabulary—mood
Look at the picture on page 7. Can you tell what mood each kid is in?
(Ruth Rose is excited. Josh is happy. Dink is nervous . . . )

*8*

around and screamed into the house. "THE GUYS ARE HERE, MOM. I'M LEAVING!"

Dink and Josh covered their ears.

"Geez, Ruth Rose," Josh said. "I don't know what's louder, your outfit or your voice."

Ruth Rose smiled sweetly at Josh.

"I can't wait until Wallis Wallace signs my book!" she said. She held up a copy of *The Phantom in the Pharmacy*.

"I wonder if Wallis Wallace will read from the new book he's working on," Dink said.

"What's the title?" Ruth Rose asked.

They headed toward the Book Nook.

"I don't know," said Dink. "But he wrote in his letter that he's doing some of the research while he's here in Connecticut."

Dink pulled the letter out of his pocket. He read it out loud while he walked.

Dear Mr. Duncan,

Thank you for your kind letter. I'm so impressed that you've read all my books! I have good news. I've made arrangements to come to the Book Nook to sign books. I can use part of my time for research. Thanks for your picture. I'm so happy to finally meet one of my most loyal fans. Short of being kidnapped, nothing will stop me from coming!

See you soon,

*Wallis Wallace*

The letter was signed *Wallis Wallace* in loopy letters. Dink grinned. "Pretty neat, huh?"

"Pretty neat, *Mister* Duncan!" teased Josh.

## After Reading Page 9

**❶ Understand:** Explaining; Using Vocabulary— impressed
What was Wallis Wallace impressed by?
(Dink had read all of his books.)
What did Wallis Wallace say was the only thing that would keep him from coming to the Book Nook?
(He said he would come unless he was kidnapped.)

**❷ Remember:** Identifying—Setting; **Apply:** Using Graphic Organizer—Map
Where do Dink, Josh, and Ruth Rose live?
(They live in Green Lawn.)
Look at the map at the beginning of the book. Point to the houses where Dink and Ruth Rose live. Good. Now find the Book Nook. Trace with your finger the quickest way for the kids to walk to the Book Nook.

10

"You should have that letter framed," Ruth Rose said.

"Great idea!" Dink said.

They passed Howard's Barbershop. Howard waved through his window as they hurried by.

"Come on!" Dink urged as he dragged his friends down the street to the Book Nook.

They looked through the window, out of breath. The bookstore was crowded with kids. The Book Nook's owner, Mr. Paskey, had set up folding chairs. Dink noticed that most of them were already taken.

Dink saw Mr. Paskey sitting behind a table. A big white sign on the table said WELCOME, WALLIS WALLACE!

But the chair behind the sign was empty. Dink gulped and stared at the empty seat.

Where was Wallis Wallace?

**After Reading Page 10**

**❶ Apply:** Predicting

Where do you think Wallis Wallace is?

(He is running late. He is waiting until it's time to start. He's been kidnapped . . . )

### CHAPTER 2 INSTRUCTIONS
Students read Chapter 2 without the teacher, independently or with partners.

### COMPREHENSION PROCESSES
**Remember, Understand, Apply**

### PROCEDURES FOR READING ON YOUR OWN

1. **Getting Ready**
   Have students turn to page 11.

2. **Setting a Purpose**

   **Identifying—Problem; Explaining; Inferring; Using Vocabulary—mood**
   Before students begin reading, say something like:
   Read to find out the answers to these questions:
   - What was the problem at the Book Nook?
   - What did Dink think might have happened? Why?
   - What was the mood in the Book Nook?

3. **Reading on Your Own: Partner or Whisper Reading**
   - Have students take turns reading every other page with a partner or have students whisper read Chapter 2 on their own.
   - Continue having students track each word with their fingers.

4. **Comprehension and Skill Work**
   Tell students they will do Case Log Entries 1a and 1b and Comprehension and Skill Activity 1 after they read on their own. Guide practice, as needed. For teacher directions, see pages 30–33.

5. **Homework 1: New Passage**

> **PREP NOTE**
> **Setting a Purpose**
> Write questions on a chalkboard, white board, or large piece of paper before working with your small group.

Dink raced into the Book Nook. Josh and Ruth Rose were right behind him. They found three seats behind Tommy Tomko and Eddie Carini.

Dink plopped his pack on the floor. The clock over the cash register said three minutes after eleven.

"Where is he?" Dink whispered to Tommy Tomko.

Tommy turned around. "Beats me. He's not here yet, and Mr. Paskey looks worried."

"What's going on?" Ruth Rose said.

*11*

*12*

Dink told her and Josh what Tommy had said.

"Paskey does look pretty nervous," Josh whispered.

"Mr. Paskey always looks nervous," Dink whispered back, looking around the room. He saw about thirty kids he knew. Mrs. Davis, Dink's neighbor, was looking at gardening books.

Dink checked out the other grownups in the store. None of them looked like a famous mystery writer.

Mr. Paskey stood up. "Boys and girls, welcome to the Book Nook! Wallis Wallace should be here any second. How many of you have books to be autographed?"

Everyone waved a book in the air.

"Wonderful! I'm sure Wallis Wallace will be happy to know that Green Lawn is a reading town!"

The kids clapped and cheered.

Dink glanced at the clock. Five past eleven. He swallowed, trying to stay calm. Wallis Wallace was late, but it was only by five minutes.

Slowly, five more minutes passed. Dink felt his palms getting damp. *Where* is *Wallis Wallace?* he wondered.

Some of the kids started getting restless. Dink heard one kid say, "Whenever *I'm* late, I get grounded!"

"So where is he?" Josh asked.

Ruth Rose looked at her watch. "It's only ten after," she said. "Famous people are always late."

Now Dink stared at the clock. The big hand jerked forward, paused, then wobbled forward again.

At 11:15, Mr. Paskey stood up again. "I don't understand why Wallis Wallace is late," he said. Dink noticed that his bald head was shiny with sweat. His bow tie was getting a workout.

Mr. Paskey smiled bravely, but his eyes were blinking like crazy through his thick glasses. "Shall we give him a few more minutes?"

The crowd grumbled, but nobody wanted to go anywhere.

Ruth Rose started to read her book.

Josh opened his sketch pad and began drawing Mr. Paskey. Dink turned and stared at the door. He mentally ordered Wallis Wallace to walk through it. *You have to come!* thought Dink.

*16*

Ever since he had received Wallis Wallace's letter, he'd thought about only one thing: meeting him today.

Suddenly Dink felt his heart skip a beat. THE LETTER! *Short of being kidnapped,* the letter said, *nothing will stop me from coming.*

*Kidnapped!* Dink shook himself. Of course Wallis Wallace hadn't been kidnapped!

Mr. Paskey stood again, but this time he wasn't smiling. "I'm sorry, kids," he said. "But Wallis Wallace doesn't seem to be coming after all."

The kids groaned. They got up, scraping chairs and bumping knees. Mr. Paskey apologized to them as they crowded past, heading for the door.

"I've read every single one of his books," Dink heard Amy Flower tell another girl. "Now I'll probably *never* meet anyone famous!"

"I can't believe we gave up a soccer game for this!" Tommy Tomko muttered to Eddie Carini on their way out.

Ruth Rose and Josh went next, but Dink remained in his seat. He was too stunned to move.

He felt the letter through his jeans. *Short of being kidnapped...* Finally Dink got up and walked out.

Josh and Ruth Rose were waiting for him.

"What's the matter?" Ruth Rose said. "You look sick!"

"I *am* sick," Dink mumbled. "I invited him here. It's all my fault."

"What's all your fault?" Josh asked.

"This!" he said, thrusting the letter into Josh's hands. "Wallis Wallace has been *kidnapped!*"

## ENTRY 1a

### COMPREHENSION PROCESSES

Remember, Understand, Create

### WRITING TRAITS

Conventions—Complete Sentence, Capital, Question Mark
Presentation

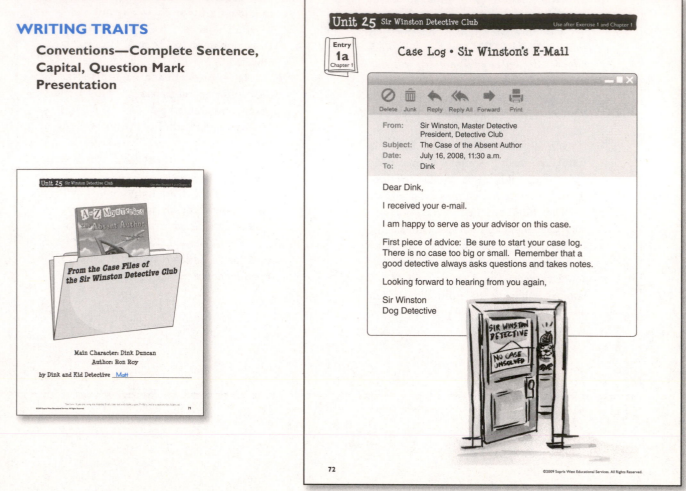

### PROCEDURES

Discuss each step. Then have students complete the page independently.

1. **Cover and E-Mail—Specific Instructions** (Entry 1a)
   • Introduce the Case Log and have students write their name on the cover.
   • Have students read the e-mail.

**ENTRY 1b**

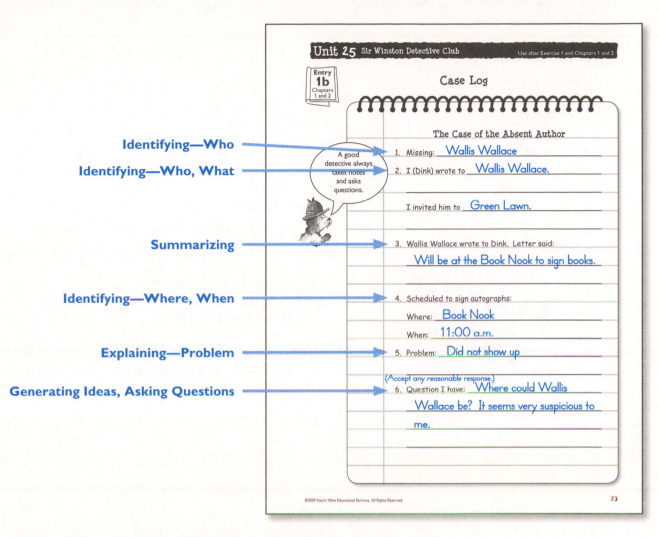

Labels (left side, pointing to Case Log items):

- Identifying—Who
- Identifying—Who, What
- Summarizing
- Identifying—Where, When
- Explaining—Problem
- Generating Ideas, Asking Questions

Case Log content:

**Unit 25** Sir Winston Detective Club · Use after Exercise 1 and Chapters 1 and 2

Entry 1b · Chapters 1 and 2

## Case Log

A good detective always takes notes and asks questions.

The Case of the Absent Author

1. Missing: Wallis Wallace
2. I (Dink) wrote to Wallis Wallace.

   I invited him to Green Lawn.

3. Wallis Wallace wrote to Dink. Letter said:

   Will be at the Book Nook to sign books.

4. Scheduled to sign autographs:

   Where: Book Nook

   When: 11:00 a.m.

5. Problem: Did not show up

   (Accept any reasonable response.)
6. Question I have: Where could Wallis Wallace be? It seems very suspicious to me.

©2009 Sopris West Educational Services. All Rights Reserved.                                    73

1. **Note Taking: Sentence Completion, Summarizing—Specific Instructions** (Items 1–5)
   Have students read each item and fill in the blanks.

2. **Note Taking: Asking Questions—Specific Instructions** (Item 6)
   Have students brainstorm questions they have about the story, then write one question in the blank. Remind students to start their question with a capital and end with a question mark.

## MYSTERY CHARACTERS

### COMPREHENSION PROCESSES
Understand, Apply

### WRITING TRAITS
Word Choice
Conventions—Complete Sentence, Capital, Period
Presentation

### PROCEDURES
Have students complete the page independently. Guide practice, only as needed.

1. **Answering Questions—Specific Instructions**
   - Have students read the clues, then fill in the blanks with the correct person.
   - Have students draw a picture of the character's face in the box.

2. **Characterization: Paragraph Writing—Specific Instructions**
   - Have students write two sentences about the main character that would help someone figure out who he or she is. Have students brainstorm ideas, if needed. Remind them to start sentences with a capital and end with a period.
   - Have students draw a picture of the main character's face in the box.

**Inferring—Who**
**Illustrating**

**Summarizing—**
**Character Traits**
**(Characterization)**
**Sentence Writing**
**Illustrating**

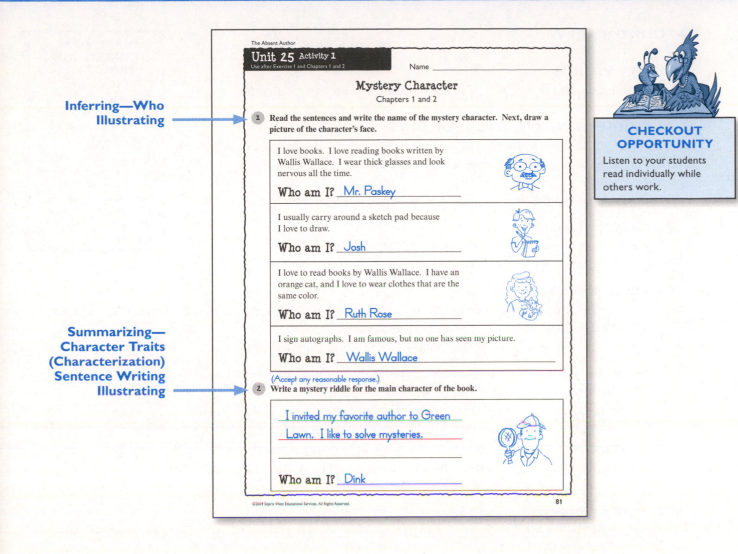

The Absent Author

**Unit 25** **Activity 1**
Use after Exercise 1 and Chapters 1 and 2

Name _____

## Mystery Character
Chapters 1 and 2

1. Read the sentences and write the name of the mystery character. Next, draw a picture of the character's face.

I love books. I love reading books written by Wallis Wallace. I wear thick glasses and look nervous all the time.

Who am I? __Mr. Paskey__

I usually carry around a sketch pad because I love to draw.

Who am I? __Josh__

I love to read books by Wallis Wallace. I have an orange cat, and I love to wear clothes that are the same color.

Who am I? __Ruth Rose__

I sign autographs. I am famous, but no one has seen my picture.

Who am I? __Wallis Wallace__

(Accept any reasonable response.)

2. Write a mystery riddle for the main character of the book.

__I invited my favorite author to Green__
__Lawn. I like to solve mysteries.__

Who am I? __Dink__

©2009 Sopris West Educational Services. All Rights Reserved.

81

### CHECKOUT OPPORTUNITY
Listen to your students read individually while others work.

**❶ SOUND REVIEW**

**❷ SHIFTY WORDS**

Have students read the words. Use the words in sentences, as needed.

**❸ ACCURACY AND FLUENCY BUILDING**

- For each task, have students say any underlined part, then read the word.
- Set a pace. Then have students read the whole words in each task and column.
- Provide repeated practice, building accuracy first, then fluency.

**B1. Contractions**

- Prompt students to tell you what a contraction is.
- Have students read the words, then the contraction.

**C1. Multisyllabic Words**

- For the list of words divided by syllables, have students read each syllable, then the whole word. Use the word in a sentence, as appropriate.
- For the list of whole words, build accuracy and then fluency.

| | |
|---|---|
| **accomplice** | The thief didn't commit the crime alone. He had an . . . *accomplice.* |
| **pardon** | Excuse me. I beg your . . . *pardon.* |
| **itinerary** | The businessman never left town without his schedule, or . . . *itinerary.* |
| **rational** | It just didn't make sense. His decision wasn't . . . *rational.* |
| **ransom** | The kidnappers returned the puppy when they were paid money, or a . . . *ransom.* |
| **suspicious** | Josh saw a man sneaking around the side of the building. The man looked . . . *suspicious.* |

**D1. Tricky Words**

- For each Tricky Word, have students use the sounds and word parts they know to silently sound out the word. Use the word in a sentence to help with pronunciation.
- If the word is unfamiliar, tell students the word.

**peculiar**
Look at the first word. Say the word parts silently. Thumbs up when you know the word.
Use my sentence to help you pronounce the word.
Something that is odd or out of the ordinary is . . . *peculiar.*
Read the word three times. (peculiar, peculiar, peculiar)

| | |
|---|---|
| **earlier** | Maya wanted to beat Ben to the school bus, so she got up . . . *earlier* . . . than usual. |
| **signing** | The author was late for his book . . . *signing.* |
| **thoughts** | What do you think of my idea? What are your . . . *thoughts?* |

- Have students go back and read the whole words in the column.

**❹ WORD ENDINGS**

**❺ NAMES AND PLACES**

**❻ MORPHOGRAPHS AND AFFIXES**

- Have students read the underlined part, then the whole word.
- Repeat practice with whole words, mixing group and individual turns. Build accuracy, then fluency.

---

> **SHIFTY WORDS CORRECTION PROCEDURE**
> **(Reminder)**
>
> If students make an error, put the word on the board. Underline the incorrect sound.
>
> Have students identify the difficult sound, then sound the word out smoothly. Have students read the row again. Return to the difficult word for three correct responses.

**❼ GENERALIZATION: READING NEW WORDS IN PARAGRAPHS**

- Have students read the paragraph silently, then out loud. Tell students to use the sounds and word parts they know to read any difficult words.
- Repeat practice, as needed.

The Absent Author

## Unit 25  Exercise 2
Use before Chapter 3

1. **SOUND REVIEW**  Use selected Sound Cards from Units 1–19.

2. **SHIFTY WORDS**  Have students read the words.

| Dink | sink | rink | rank | rang |
|------|------|------|------|------|

3. **ACCURACY/FLUENCY BUILDING**  For each column, have students say any underlined part, then read each word. Next, have them read the column.

| A1 Mixed Practice | B1 Contractions | C1 Multisyllabic Words | | D1 Tricky Words |
|------|------|------|------|------|
| gesture | that will | ac•com•plice | accomplice | peculiar |
| moose | that'll | par•don | pardon | earlier |
| hotel | he would | i•tin•e•rar•y | itinerary | signing |
| scarf | he'd | ra•tion•al | rational | thoughts |
| officer | | ran•som | ransom | |
| | | sus•pi•cious | suspicious | |

4. **WORD ENDINGS**  Have students read each underlined word, then the word with an ending.

| Ⓐ | writers | blushed | grinning | communicates | shrieked |
|---|---------|---------|----------|--------------|----------|
| Ⓑ | | bounce  bouncing | | tremble  trembly | |

5. **NAMES AND PLACES**  Have students use the sounds and word parts they know to figure out the words.

| Bradley Airport | New England Airlines | Jimmy Fallon |
|-----------------|----------------------|--------------|

6. **MORPHOGRAPHS AND AFFIXES**  Have students read each underlined part, then the word.

| nervously | shyly | conclusion | explanation |
|-----------|-------|------------|-------------|

7. **GENERALIZATION**  Have students read the paragraph silently, then out loud.  (New words: Grampa's, absence, practically, handkerchief)

After Grampa's long absence, Wallace was practically bursting to see him.  Finally, Grampa stepped off the plane.  Wallace raced to hug him.  Tears of joy streamed down Grampa's face.  He took out his handkerchief and blew his nose.  "I sure am happy to see you," said Grampa.

---

**BUILDING MASTERY WITH JAZZY PRACTICE (Reminder)**

For variety, practice underlined sounds in a jazzy rhythm. Say something like: Listen to me do Column A1 in a rhythm. I'm going to quickly say each underlined sound two times and then read the word.
/ge/, /ge/, gesture; /o͞o/, /o͞o/, moose; /ō͞ō/, /ō͞ō/, hotel.

Your turn. Start at the top of Column A1 and keep going.
(/ge/, /ge/, gesture; /o͞o/, /o͞o/, moose; /ō͞ō/, /ō͞ō/, hotel . . . )

## COMPREHENSION PROCESSES

Apply, Analyze

## PROCEDURES

**Introducing Vocabulary**

★ **gesture, mention** ★ **peculiar** ★ **suspicious** ★ **accomplice** ★ **itinerary**

- For each vocabulary word, have students read the word by parts, then read the whole word.
- Read the student-friendly explanations to students as they follow with their fingers. Then have students use the vocabulary word by following the gray text.
- Review and discuss the illustrations.
  *Note*: Student vocabulary pages for this unit are found in the students' *Exercise Book 4*.

The Absent Author

**Unit 25** Vocabulary 2
Use after Exercise 2

**USING VOCABULARY**

| ★**ges•ture**<br><br>A **gesture** is an action that communicates something without talking. People gesture with their heads and hands. | The teacher *gestured* to the class to quiet down.<br><br>Show me what kind of gesture the teacher might have made. **1** | |
|---|---|---|
| **men•tion**<br><br>**Mention** means to say or write a little about something. | Isabel *mentioned* that she will be going to Mexico next summer.<br><br>Did she say a lot about her trip? **2** | ...blah, blah blah...oh, and did I mention... |
| ★**pe•cu•liar**<br><br>Something **peculiar** is strange. | There was a *peculiar* smell in the kitchen.<br><br>Describe the smell. **3** | SNIFF SNIFF |

**1 Apply:** Demonstrating; Using Vocabulary—gesture
**2 Apply:** Using Vocabulary—mention (No, she only mentioned it. She said a little bit.)
**3 Apply:** Using Vocabulary—peculiar (The smell was strange.)

★ = New in this unit

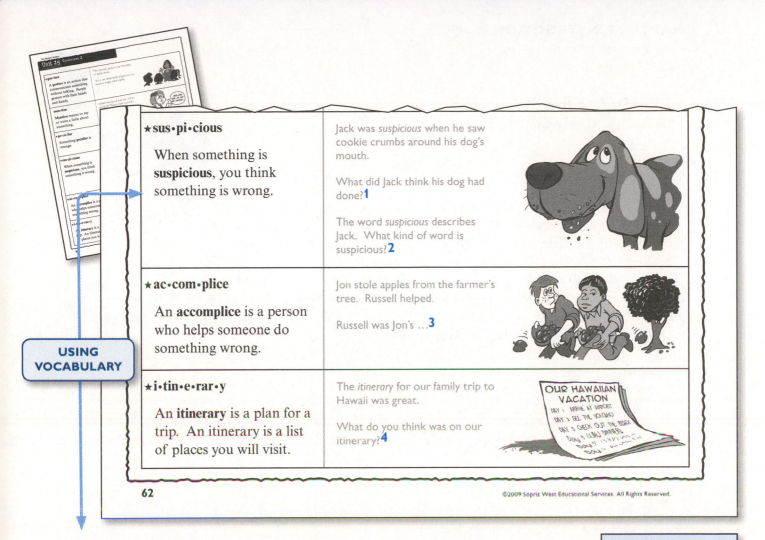

USING VOCABULARY

★sus•pi•cious

When something is **suspicious**, you think something is wrong.

Jack was *suspicious* when he saw cookie crumbs around his dog's mouth.

What did Jack think his dog had done?**1**

The word *suspicious* describes Jack. What kind of word is suspicious?**2**

★ac•com•plice

An **accomplice** is a person who helps someone do something wrong.

Jon stole apples from the farmer's tree. Russell helped.

Russell was Jon's ...**3**

★i•tin•e•rar•y

An **itinerary** is a plan for a trip. An itinerary is a list of places you will visit.

The *itinerary* for our family trip to Hawaii was great.

What do you think was on our itinerary?**4**

OUR HAWAIIAN VACATION
DAY 1  ARRIVE AT AIRPORT
DAY 2  SEE THE VOLCANO
DAY 3  CHECK OUT THE BEACH
DAY 4  LUAU DINNER

62

❶ **Apply:** Using Vocabulary—suspicious (Jack thought his dog had eaten the cookies. Jack thought his dog had done something wrong.)

❷ **Analyze:** Classifying; **Apply:** Using Vocabulary—suspicious (Suspicious is an adjective.)

❸ **Apply:** Using Vocabulary—accomplice (accomplice)

❹ **Apply:** Using Vocabulary—itinerary (Your itinerary might have had surfing, scuba diving, and visiting volcanoes.)

**USING VOCABULARY**

Be enthusiastic about learning new words. Keep a running list of words you would like to use and encourage students to use. Keep the list handy when you are teaching. Put students' names on the board to acknowledge use of a word. Say things like:

Wow! [Greg] used the word *peculiar* when he talked about the strange way his dog was acting. That's a great way to use a vocabulary word!

## CHAPTER 3 INSTRUCTIONS

Students read Chapter 3, pages 18–23 with the teacher and pages 24–27 on their own.

## COMPREHENSION PROCESSES

**Remember, Understand, Apply, Analyze**

## PROCEDURES

1. **Reviewing Chapter 2**

   **Summarizing; Identifying—Problem; Inferring; Using Vocabulary— mood, restless, disappointed**

   Have students turn to page 11. Quickly discuss the questions from Chapter 2, Setting a Purpose. Say something like:

   Yesterday, you read Chapter 2 on your own. Let's see what you found out.
   What was the problem at the Book Nook? (Wallis Wallace didn't show up for the book signing.)
   What did Dink think might have happened?
   (He thought the author might have been kidnapped.)
   Why? (In his letter, Wallace said "Short of being kidnapped . . . ")
   What was the mood in the Book Nook?
   (The kids were restless, disappointed, maybe a little mad . . . )

2. **Introducing Chapter 3, pages 18–23**

   **Predicting**

   Say something like:

   At the end of Chapter 2, Dink said he thought Wallis had been kidnapped.
   What do you think will happen next?
   (They will call the police.  The kids will start to investigate . . . )

3. **First Reading**
   - Ask questions and discuss the story as indicated by the blue text in this guide.
   - Mix group and individual turns, independent of your voice.
     Have students work toward a group accuracy goal of 0–6 errors.
     Quietly keep track of errors made by all students in the group.
   - After reading the story, practice any difficult words.
     Reread the story if students have not reached the accuracy goal.

4. **Second Reading, Timed Readings: Repeated Reading**

   - As time allows, have students do Timed Readings while others follow along.
   - Time individuals for 30 seconds and encourage each child to work for a personal best.
   - Determine words correct per minute. Record student scores.

## Chapter 3

"KIDNAPPED?" Ruth Rose shrieked. Her blue eyes were huge.

Josh and Dink covered their ears.

"Shh!" said Josh. He handed the letter back to Dink and gave a quick gesture with his head. "Some strange woman is watching us!"

*18*

Dink had noticed the woman earlier. She'd been sitting in the back of the Book Nook.

"She's coming over here!" Ruth Rose said.

The woman had brown hair up in a neat bun. Half-glasses perched on her

20

nose. She was wearing a brown dress and brown shoes, and carried a book bag with a picture of a moose on the side. Around her neck she wore a red scarf covered with tiny black letters.

"Excuse me," she said in a soft, trembly voice. "Did you say Wallis Wallace has been *kidnapped?*" The woman poked her glasses nervously.

Dink wasn't sure what to say. He *thought* Wallis Wallace had been kidnapped, but he couldn't be sure. Finally he said, "Well, he might have been."

"My goodness!" gasped the woman.

"Who are you?" Josh asked her.

"Oh, pardon me!" The woman blushed. "My name is Mavis Green," she mumbled. "I'm a writer, and I came to meet Mr. Wallace."

Dink said, "I'm Dink Duncan. These are my friends Ruth Rose and Josh."

Mavis shook hands shyly.

Then she reached into her book bag and pulled out a folded paper.

"Wallis Wallace wrote to me last week. He said something very peculiar in his letter. I didn't think much of it at the time. But when he didn't show up today, and then I heard you mention kidnapping…"

She handed the letter to Dink. Josh and Ruth Rose read it over his shoulder.

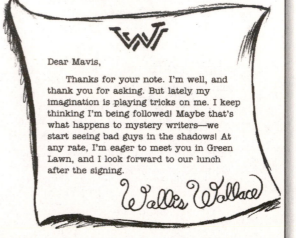

Dear Mavis,

Thanks for your note. I'm well, and thank you for asking. But lately my imagination is playing tricks on me. I keep thinking I'm being followed! Maybe that's what happens to mystery writers—we start seeing bad guys in the shadows! At any rate, I'm eager to meet you in Green Lawn, and I look forward to our lunch after the signing.

*Wallis Wallace*

### After Reading Pages 18–20

**❶ Understand:** Describing
Describe Mavis Green.
(She was a writer who came to meet Wallis Wallace. She had on a brown dress and brown shoes. She had brown hair and glasses. She carried a bag with a moose on it, and she wore a scarf with little black letters.)

### After Reading Page 21

**❶ Understand:** Explaining
Why did Mavis Green think Wallis Wallace may have been kidnapped?
(In a letter to her, he said that he thought he was being followed.)

**❷ Analyze:** Comparing; **Apply:** Using Vocabulary—mention, suspicious
What was the same about Dink's letter and Mavis's letter from Wallis Wallace?
(Both letters have two W's at the top. The signatures look the same. They both mention something suspicious.)

22

"Wow!" said Ruth Rose. "First he says he's being followed, and then he winds up missing!"

Dink told Mavis about his letter from Wallis Wallace. "He said the only thing that would keep him from coming today was if he was kidnapped!"

"Oh, dear!" said Mavis. "I just don't understand. Why would anyone want to kidnap Wallis Wallace?"

"If he's the most famous mystery writer in the world, he must be rich, right?" Josh said. "Maybe someone kidnapped him for a ransom!"

Suddenly Josh grabbed Dink and spun him around, pointing toward the street. "Look! The cops are coming! They must have heard about the kidnapping!"

A police officer was walking toward them.

"Josh, that's just Officer Fallon,

Jimmy Fallon's grandfather," said Dink. "Jimmy came to get a book signed. I saw him inside the Book Nook."

"Maybe we should show Officer Fallon these letters," Ruth Rose suggested. "They could be clues if Wallis Wallace has really been kidnapped!"

"Who's been kidnapped?" asked Officer Fallon, who was now standing near them. "Not my grandson, I hope," he added, grinning.

Dink showed Officer Fallon the two letters. "We think Wallis Wallace might have been kidnapped," he said. "He promised he'd come to sign books, but he isn't here."

Officer Fallon read Mavis's letter first, then Dink's. He scratched his chin, then handed the letters back.

"The letters do sound a bit suspicious," he said. "But it's more likely that Mr. Wallace just missed his flight."

## After Reading Pages 22–23

**❶ Analyze:** Drawing Conclusions
Do you think Wallis Wallace was kidnapped? Why or why not?
(Yes, Wallis Wallace was worried about being kidnapped . . . )

**❷ Understand:** Defining and Using Vocabulary—suspicious
Officer Fallon thinks the letters sound a bit suspicious, but he doesn't seem to be worried. What does *suspicious* mean?
(The letters could be a sign that something is wrong.)

**❸ Understand:** Explaining
Why did Officer Fallon think Wallis Wallace didn't show up?
(He thought Wallis Wallace missed his flight.)

## CHAPTER 3 INSTRUCTIONS
Students read Chapter 3, pages 24–27, without the teacher, independently or with partners.

## COMPREHENSION PROCESSES
**Remember, Understand, Apply, Create**

## PROCEDURES FOR READING ON YOUR OWN

1. **Getting Ready**
   Have students turn to page 24.

2. **Setting a Purpose**

   **Identifying—Where; Inferring; Explaining; Generating Ideas**
   Before students begin reading, say something like:
   As you read the next pages, try to answer these questions:
   - Where did the kids start looking for Wallace?
   - Why do you think Mr. Paskey was nervous?
   - How did Mr. Paskey help the kids?
   - What do you think the kids should do next?

> **PREP NOTE**
> **Setting a Purpose**
> Write questions on a chalkboard, white board, or large piece of paper before working with your small group.

3. **Reading on Your Own: Partner or Whisper Reading**
   - Have students take turns reading every other page with a partner or have students whisper read pages 24–27 on their own.
   - Continue having students track each word with their fingers.

4. **Comprehension and Skill Work**
   Tell students they will do Case Log Entry 2 and Comprehension and Skill Activity 2 after they read on their own. Guide practice, as needed. For teacher directions, see pages 45 and 46.

5. **Homework 2: New Passage**

24

Jimmy Fallon ran out of the Book Nook, waving a Wallis Wallace book at his grandfather. "Grampa, he never came! Can we go for ice cream anyway?"

Officer Fallon put a big hand on Jimmy's head. "In a minute, son." To Dink he said, "I wouldn't worry. Mr. Wallace will turn up. Call me tomorrow if there's no news, okay?"

They watched Jimmy and his grandfather walk away.

Dink handed Mavis's letter back to her. He folded his and slid it into his pocket. Crazy thoughts were bouncing around in his head. *What if Wallis Wallace really has been kidnapped? It happened because I invited him to Green Lawn. I'm practically an accomplice!*

"I don't want to wait till tomorrow," he said finally. "I say we start looking for Wallis Wallace now!"

"Where do we start?" Ruth Rose asked.

Dink jerked his thumb over his shoulder. "Right here at the Book Nook."

"Excuse me," Mavis Green said shyly. "May I come along, too?"

"Sure," Dink said. He marched back inside the Book Nook, with the others following.

Mr. Paskey was putting the Wallis Wallace books back on a shelf. He looked even more nervous than before.

"Excuse me, Mr. Paskey," Dink said. "Have you heard from Wallis Wallace?"

Mr. Paskey's hand shot up to his bow tie. "No, Dink, not a word."

"We think he was kidnapped!" Josh said.

Mr. Paskey swallowed, making his bow tie wiggle. "Now, Joshua, let's not jump to conclusions. I'm sure there's a

26

rational explanation for his absence."

Dink told Mr. Paskey about the two letters. "I'm really worried, Mr. Paskey. Where could he be?"

Mr. Paskey took out a handkerchief and wiped his face. "I have no idea." He removed a paper from his desk and handed it to Dink. "All I have is his itinerary."

The others looked over Dink's shoulder as he read:

**Itinerary for Wallis Wallace:**

1. Arrive at Bradley Airport at 7:00 P.M., Friday, July 15, New England Airlines, Flight 3132.
2. Meet driver from Lawrence Taxi Service.
3. Drive to Shangri-La Hotel.
4. Sign books at Book Nook at 11:00 A.M., Saturday, July 16.
5. Lunch, then back to airport for 4:30 P.M. flight.

"Can I keep this?" Dink asked Mr. Paskey.

Mr. Paskey blinked. "Well, I guess that'll be all right. But why do you need the itinerary?"

Dink picked up a marker and drew circles around the words AIRPORT, TAXI, HOTEL, and BOOK NOOK.

"This is like a trail. It leads from the airport last night to the Book Nook today," Dink said. "Somewhere along this trail, Wallis Wallace disappeared."

Dink stared at the itinerary. "And we're going to find him!"

## ENTRY 2

### COMPREHENSION PROCESSES

Understand, Apply

### WRITING TRAITS

Conventions—Period

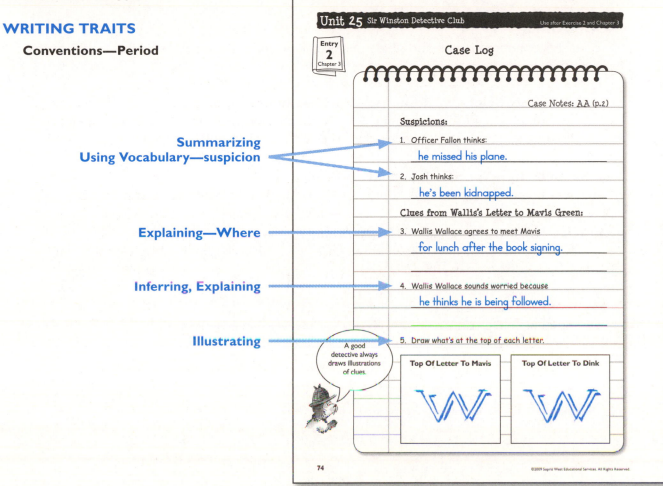

Summarizing
Using Vocabulary—suspicion

Explaining—Where

Inferring, Explaining

Illustrating

## PROCEDURES

Discuss each step. Then have students complete the page independently.

1. **Note Taking: Summarizing, Sentence Completion—Basic Instructions** (Items 1–4)
   Have students read each item and fill in the blanks. Remind them to put a period at the end of sentences, where appropriate.

2. **Illustrating—Specific Instructions** (Item 5)
   Have students draw the logo at the top of each letter from Wallis Wallace.

### STORY COMPREHENSION

### COMPREHENSION PROCESSES

**Remember, Understand, Analyze**

### PROCEDURES

For each step, demonstrate and guide practice, as needed. Then have students complete the page independently.

1. **True/False: Selection Response—Specific Instructions** (Item 1)
   Have students read the directions. Have students read each item in the chart, determine whether the item is true or false, then check the correct box.

2. **Sequencing—Specific Instructions** (Item 2)
   Have students read the directions, then fill in the blanks with the correct itinerary.

3. **Selection Response—Basic Instructions** (Items 3, 4)
   Have students read questions and sentences and fill in the bubble or check the blanks with the correct answer(s).

*Self-monitoring*
Have students check and correct their work.

**Identifying—What**
**Test Taking**

**Sequencing—Events**

**Identifying—Who**

**Comparing**
**Drawing Conclusions**

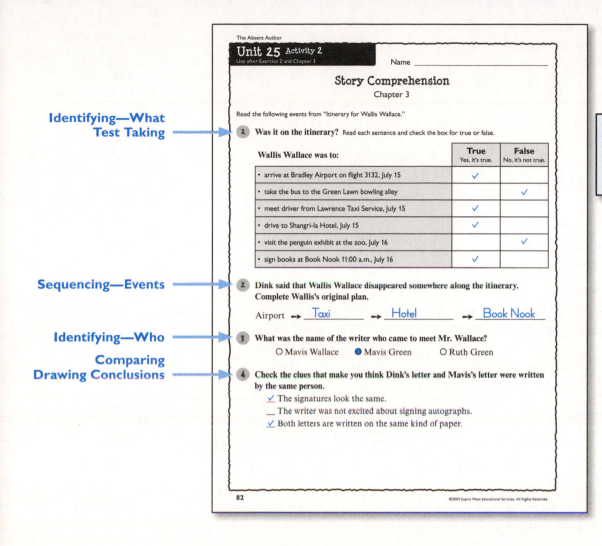

The Absent Author

**Unit 25** Activity 2
Use after Exercise 2 and Chapter 3

Name _____

## Story Comprehension
### Chapter 3

Read the following events from "Itinerary for Wallis Wallace."

**1** **Was it on the itinerary?** Read each sentence and check the box for true or false.

| Wallis Wallace was to: | True<br>Yes, it's true. | False<br>No, it's not true. |
|---|---|---|
| • arrive at Bradley Airport on flight 3132, July 15 | ✓ | |
| • take the bus to the Green Lawn bowling alley | | ✓ |
| • meet driver from Lawrence Taxi Service, July 15 | ✓ | |
| • drive to Shangri-la Hotel, July 15 | ✓ | |
| • visit the penguin exhibit at the zoo, July 16 | | ✓ |
| • sign books at Book Nook 11:00 a.m., July 16 | ✓ | |

**2** **Dink said that Wallis Wallace disappeared somewhere along the itinerary.**
**Complete Wallis's original plan.**

Airport → __Taxi__ → __Hotel__ → __Book Nook__

**3** **What was the name of the writer who came to meet Mr. Wallace?**
   ○ Mavis Wallace   ● Mavis Green   ○ Ruth Green

**4** **Check the clues that make you think Dink's letter and Mavis's letter were written**
**by the same person.**
   ✓ The signatures look the same.
   _ The writer was not excited about signing autographs.
   ✓ Both letters are written on the same kind of paper.

82

**CHECKOUT**
**OPPORTUNITY**
Listen to your students
read individually while
others work.

### ① SHIFTY WORDS

Have students read the words. Use the words in sentences, as needed.

### ② ACCURACY AND FLUENCY BUILDING

- For each task, have students say any underlined part, then read the word.
- Set a pace. Then have students read the whole words in each task and column.
- Provide repeated practice, building accuracy first, then fluency.

#### B1. Compound Words

Ask students what a compound word is. Then have them read the words.

#### C1. Multisyllabic Words

Have students read each whole word. Use each word in a sentence, as needed.

#### E1. Tricky Words

- For each Tricky Word, have students use the sounds and word parts they know to silently sound out the word. Use the word in a sentence to help with pronunciation.

| | |
|---|---|
| **shoulder** | Lara fell and hurt her . . . *shoulder.* |
| **castle** | The king and queen lived in a huge stone . . . *castle.* |
| **woman** | The opposite of man is . . . *woman.* |
| **wondered** | Stink was really curious. He . . . *wondered* . . . about everything. |
| **merry** | He was a very jolly man. He was . . . *merry.* |
| **merriest** | Miss Tam is the most delightful person we know. She is the . . . *merriest* . . . person we know. |

- Have students go back and read the whole words in the column.

### ③ MULTISYLLABIC WORDS

For each word, have students read the syllables, then the whole word. Use the word in a sentence, as appropriate.

| | |
|---|---|
| **celebrity** | Judith is a famous actress. She is a . . . *celebrity.* |
| **itinerary** | What's your schedule, or . . . *itinerary?* |
| **reflected** | The mirror . . . *reflected* . . . her image. |
| **lobby** | They checked in at the hotel . . . *lobby.* |
| **guilty** | Even though Evan didn't take the money, his neighbor thought he was . . . *guilty.* |
| **previous** | What kind of job did you do before? What was your . . . *previous* . . . job? |

### ④ WORDS IN CONTEXT

For each word, have students use the sounds and word parts they know to silently sound out the word. Then have students read the sentence. Assist, as needed.

### ⑤ NAMES AND PLACES

Have students use the sounds and word parts they know to figure out the words. Use the words in sentences, as needed.

### ⑥ GENERALIZATION: READING NEW WORDS IN PARAGRAPHS

- Have students read the paragraph silently, then out loud. Tell students to use the sounds and word parts they know to read any difficult words.
- Repeat practice, as needed.

> **MULTISYLLABIC WORDS CORRECTION PROCEDURE**
>
> If students make an error, put the word on the board. Draw loops under each syllable and guide practice with your hand. Have students say each syllable then read the whole word.

The Absent Author

## Unit 25 Exercise 3
Use before Chapter 4

**1. SHIFTY WORDS** Have students read the words.

| | | | | |
|---|---|---|---|---|
| chat | cat | cab | cap | cop |

**2. ACCURACY/FLUENCY BUILDING** For each column, have students say any underlined part, then read each word. Next, have them read the column.

| **A1**<br>Mixed Practice | **B1**<br>Compound Words | **C1**<br>Multisyllabic Words | **D1**<br>Word Endings | **E1**<br>Tricky Words |
|---|---|---|---|---|
| sp<u>oo</u>ky | strawberry | consider | <u>drivers</u> | shoulder |
| c<u>oi</u>ns | clipboard | swallowing | <u>kidnapper</u> | castle |
| sw<u>ea</u>ting | crossword | napkin | <u>crunching</u> | woman |
| sq<u>u</u>inted | **B2**<br>Rhyming Words | mayonnaise | <u>scooting</u> | wondered |
| sm<u>ea</u>red | die | responsible | <u>shooed</u> | |
| n<u>o</u>pe | pie | | | merry |
| grass<u>y</u> | tie | | | merriest |

**3. MULTISYLLABIC WORDS** Have students read each word part, then read each whole word.

| | | | | |
|---|---|---|---|---|
| Ⓐ | ce·leb·ri·ty | celebrity | i·tin·e·rar·y | itinerary |
| Ⓑ | re·flec·ted | reflected | lob·by | lobby |
| Ⓒ | guil·ty | guilty | pre·vi·ous | previous |

**4. WORDS IN CONTEXT** Have students use the sounds they know and then the sentence to pronounce each undelined word.

| | | |
|---|---|---|
| Ⓐ | e·on | An <u>eon</u> is an extremely long time. |
| Ⓑ | pi·sta·chi·o | My favorite kind of nut is a <u>pistachio</u>. |

**5. NAMES AND PLACES** Have students use the sounds and word parts they know to figure out the words.

| | | |
|---|---|---|
| Marilyn Monroe | Maureen Higgins | Shangri-la Hotel |

**6. GENERALIZATION** Have students read the paragraph silently, then out loud. (New words: o'clock, mustard, triple-decker, ketchup, oozed)

Josh and Adam met at the diner at 12 o'clock. Josh ordered a hot dog with mustard. Adam ordered a triple-decker hamburger with onions, lettuce, bacon, and ketchup. When he took a bite, ketchup oozed out and fell on his shirt.

63

---

**APPROPRIATE CORRECTIONS**
(Reminder)

Write any difficult words on a board or clipboard.

**Single-Syllable Pattern Words**

Have students identify the difficult sound, then sound out and say the word.

**Multisyllabic Words**

Draw loops under each word part and then guide practice with your hand.

**Tricky Words**

Have students sound out or read the word by parts, then say the word. Next have students say, spell, and say the word.

After gently correcting a word with the group, go on to other tasks or words. Return to the difficult word at least three times.

## COMPREHENSION PROCESSES

Understand, Apply

## PROCEDURES

**Introducing Vocabulary**

recognize ★ suspect ★ previous ★ celebrity

- For each vocabulary word, have students read the word by parts, then read the whole word.
- Read the student-friendly explanations to students as they follow with their fingers. Then have students use the vocabulary word by following the gray text.
- Review and discuss the illustrations.
  *Note*: Student vocabulary pages for this unit are found in the students' *Exercise Book 4*.

**USING VOCABULARY**

The Absent Author

# Unit 25 Vocabulary 3
Use after Exercise 3

**re·cog·nize**

**Recognize** means to know who someone is.

Mr. Chapman grew a mustache so we did not ...**1**

**★sus·pect**

A **suspect** is someone who people think is responsible for a crime.

Dink wondered who kidnapped Wallis Wallace. He was looking for a ...**2**

❶ **Understand:** Using Vocabulary—recognize (recognize him)
❷ **Apply:** Using Vocabulary—suspect (suspect)

★ = New in this unit

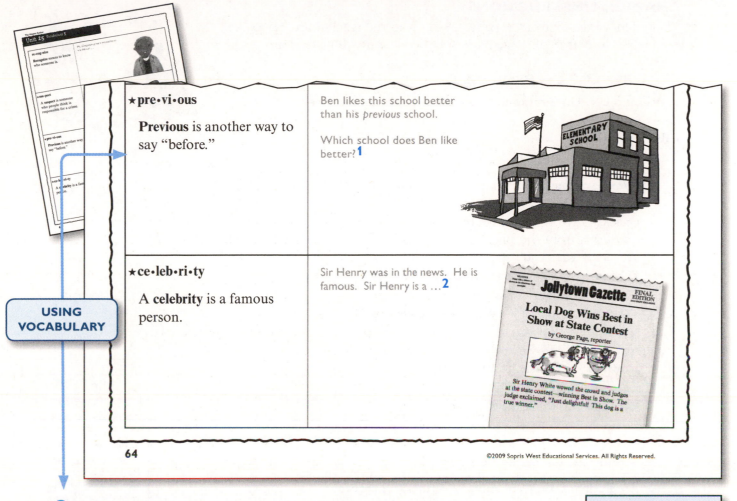

★**pre·vi·ous**

**Previous** is another way to say "before."

Ben likes this school better than his *previous* school.

Which school does Ben like better?[1]

★**ce·leb·ri·ty**

A **celebrity** is a famous person.

Sir Henry was in the news. He is famous. Sir Henry is a ...[2]

*Jollytown Gazette* FINAL EDITION

**Local Dog Wins Best in Show at State Contest**
by George Page, reporter

Sir Henry White wowed the crowd and judges at the state contest—winning Best in Show. The judge exclaimed, "Just delightful! This dog is a true winner."

64

©2009 Sopris West Educational Services. All Rights Reserved.

**USING VOCABULARY**

❶ **Understand:** Using Vocabulary—previous  (Ben likes this school better.)
❷ **Apply:** Using Vocabulary—celebrity  (celebrity)

## CHAPTER 4 INSTRUCTIONS

Students read Chapter 4, pages 28–34 with the teacher and pages 34–39 on their own. Page 34 is split between reading sessions.

## COMPREHENSION PROCESSES

**Remember, Understand, Apply, Analyze, Evaluate, Create**

## PROCEDURES

### 1. Reviewing Chapter 3

**Summarizing; Identifying—Where; Inferring; Generating Ideas; Using Vocabulary—itinerary**

Quickly review what has happened in the story so far. Discuss the questions from the previous Setting a Purpose. Say something like:

Yesterday you read pages 24–27 on your own. Let's see what you found out.

Where did the kids start looking for Wallace?

(They started at the Book Nook.)

Why do you think Mr. Paskey was so nervous?

(He was nervous because he organized the book signing and then Wallis didn't show up. Maybe he knew something about why Wallis didn't come . . . )

How did Mr. Paskey help the kids?

(He gave them the itinerary for Wallis Wallace.)

What do you think the kids should do next?

(They should follow Wallis Wallace's itinerary.)

### 2. Introducing Chapter 4

**Predicting; Using Vocabulary—itinerary, retrace**

Say something like:

What do you think will happen in this chapter?

(The kids will use the itinerary to retrace Wallis Wallace's visit to Green Lawn to figure out what happened to him . . . )

> **REPEATED READINGS**
> **Prosody**
> On the second reading, students practice developing prosody—phrasing and expression. Research has shown that prosody is related to both fluency and comprehension.

### 3. First Reading

- Ask questions and discuss the story as indicated by the blue text in this guide.
- Mix group and individual turns, independent of your voice. Have students work toward a group accuracy goal of 0–6 errors. Quietly keep track of errors made by all students in the group.
- After reading the story, practice any difficult words. Reread the story if students have not reached the accuracy goal.

### 4. Second Reading, Short Passage Practice: Developing Prosody

- Demonstrate expressive, fluent reading of the first paragraph. Read at a rate slightly faster than the students' rate.
- Guide practice with your voice.
- Provide individual turns while others track with their fingers and whisper read.
- Repeat with one paragraph at a time.

**Chapter 4**

Mr. Paskey shooed them out of the Book Nook and locked the front door. "I have to eat lunch," he said. He scurried down Main Street.

"Come on," Dink said. "There's a phone in Ellie's Diner."

"Good, we can eat while you're calling..." Josh stopped. "Who are you calling?"

"The airport," Dink said, "to see if Wallis Wallace was on that seven o'clock flight last night."

They walked into Ellie's Diner just

28

as Jimmy Fallon and his grandfather came out. Jimmy was working on a triple-decker chocolate cone.

Ellie stood behind the counter. As usual, her apron was smeared with ketchup, mustard, chocolate, and a lot of stuff Dink didn't recognize.

Ellie smiled. "Hi, Dink. Butter crunch, right?"

Dink shook his head. "No, thanks, Ellie. I came to use the phone."

"Excuse me, but would it be all right if I bought you each a cone?" Mavis Green asked. "I was going to buy lunch for Mr. Wallace anyway."

"Gee, thanks," Josh said. "I'll have a scoop of mint chip and a scoop of pistachio."

"Oh, you like green ice cream, too," Mavis said. She smiled shyly. "I'll have the same, please."

"I like pink ice cream," Ruth Rose

**After Reading Pages 28 and 29**

❶ **Understand: Explaining**
Why did Dink want to stop at Ellie's Diner?
(He wanted to call the airport to see if Wallis Wallace was on his flight last night.)

❷ **Analyze: Comparing**
What do Josh and Mavis Green have in common?
(They both like green ice cream.)

said. "I'll have a strawberry cone, please. One scoop."

"How about you, Dink?" Mavis asked.

"I'm not hungry, thanks," he said. "But you guys go ahead. I'm going to call the airport."

Dink felt guilty. If he hadn't invited Wallis Wallace to Green Lawn, his favorite author would be safe at home in his castle in Maine.

But Dink couldn't help feeling excited too. He felt like a detective from one of Wallis Wallace's books!

## After Reading Pages 30 and 31

**1 Understand:** Explaining
How did Dink feel when he was calling the airport? Why?
(He felt guilty because he invited Wallis Wallace to Green Lawn.  He also felt excited because he was trying to find Wallis, just like a real detective.)

**2 Evaluate:** Responding; **Apply:** Explaining
Would you want to be a detective and solve cases? Why or why not?
(Yes, it would be exciting to figure out the clues and solve the case.  No, it could be dangerous . . . )

*32*

Dink stepped into the phone booth, looked up the number for New England Airlines, and called. When a voice came on, he asked if Wallis Wallace had been aboard Flight 3132 last night.

"He was? Did it land at seven o'clock?" Dink asked. "Thanks a lot!"

He rushed out of the phone booth. "Hey, guys, they told me Wallis Wallace was on the plane—and it landed right on time!"

"So he didn't miss his flight," Ruth Rose said through strawberry-pink lips.

"That's right!" Dink pulled out the itinerary. He drew a line through AIRPORT.

"This is so exciting!" Ruth Rose said.

"Now what?" Josh asked, working on his double-dipper.

Dink pointed to his next circle on the itinerary. "Now we need to find out if a taxi picked him up," he said.

"Lawrence Taxi is over by the river," Ruth Rose said.

Dink looked at Mavis. "Would you like to come with us? We can walk there in five minutes."

Mavis Green wiped her lips carefully with a napkin. "I'd love to come," she said in her soft voice.

They left Ellie's Diner, walked left on Bridge Lane, then headed down Woodview Road toward the river.

"Mr. Paskey looked pretty upset, didn't he?" Josh said, crunching the last of his cone. His chin was green.

"Wouldn't you be upset if you had a bunch of customers at your store waiting to meet a famous author and he didn't show up?" Ruth Rose asked.

"Yeah, but he was sweating buckets," Josh said. "I wonder if Mr. Paskey kidnapped Wallis Wallace."

"Josh, get real! Why would Mr.

## After Reading Page 32

**❶ Understand:** Explaining—Event
What did Dink learn when he called the airline?
(Wallis Wallace was on the flight. He didn't miss his plane.)

**❷ Apply:** Using Graphic Organizer; **Understand:** Identifying—Where
Turn to the map at the beginning of the book. Where are the kids now?
(The kids are at Ellie's Diner.)
Find Ellie's Diner on the map. Where will they go next?
(Lawrence Taxi)
Find Lawrence Taxi. Now trace their route with your finger.

**❸ Create:** Generating Ideas, Asking Questions; **Apply:** Using Vocabulary—mood
If you were with the kids, what questions would you ask at the taxi company?
(Did your taxi pick up Wallis Wallace at the airport last night? Where did you take him? What was he wearing? What kind of mood was he in?)

## After Reading Page 33

**❶ Evaluate:** Responding; **Understand:** Using Vocabulary—opinion, suspect
What's your opinion? Do you think Mr. Paskey should be a suspect? Why or why not?
(Yes, I think he should be a suspect. He was sweating buckets. He was nervous. No, I don't think he should be a suspect. He was nervous because everyone was waiting for Wallis Wallace and he didn't show up.)

34

Paskey kidnap an author?" asked Ruth Rose. "He sells tons of Wallis Wallace's books!"

"I don't think Mr. Paskey is the kidnapper," Dink said. "But in a way, Josh is right. Detectives should consider everyone a suspect, just the way they do in Wallis Wallace's books."

At River Road, they turned left. Two minutes later, Dink pushed open the door of the Lawrence Taxi Service office. He asked the man behind the counter if one of their drivers had met Flight 3132 at Bradley Airport the previous night.

The man ran his finger down a list on a clipboard. "That would be Maureen Higgins. She's out back eating her lunch," he said, pointing over his shoulder. "Walk straight through."

They cut through the building to a grassy area in back. Through the trees,

**Stop Reading Here**

## After Reading Page 34, First Half

**❶ Understand:** Explaining; Using Vocabulary—suspect
Why did Ruth Rose think Mr. Paskey was not a good suspect?
(Mr. Paskey sold lots of books by Wallis Wallace . . . )

**❷ Analyze:** Drawing Conclusions
Why do you think a detective should consider everyone a suspect?
(You might miss some clues if you don't investigate everyone.  You might have the wrong suspect, and then you'll have to start over . . . )

#### CHAPTER 4 INSTRUCTIONS

Students read Chapter 4, pages 34 (last full paragraph) through 39, without the teacher, independently or with partners.

#### COMPREHENSION PROCESSES

**Understand, Apply**

#### PROCEDURES FOR READING ON YOUR OWN

**1. Getting Ready**

Have students turn to page 34 and find the last full paragraph.

**2. Setting a Purpose**

**Describing—Character Traits (Characterization); Predicting**
Before students begin reading, say something like:
Read to find out the answers to these questions:
   • How did Maureen Higgins describe Wallace?
   • Where do you think Dink and his friends will look next?

> **PREP NOTE**
> **Setting a Purpose**
> Write questions on a chalkboard, white board, or large piece of paper before working with your small group.

**3. Reading on Your Own: Partner or Whisper Reading**
   • Have students take turns reading every other page with a partner or have students whisper read pages 34–39 on their own.
   • Continue having students track each word with their fingers.

**4. Comprehension and Skill Work**

Tell students they will do Case Log Entry 3 and Comprehension and Skill Activity 3 after they read on their own. Guide practice, as needed. For teacher directions, see pages 61 and 62.

**5. Homework 3: New Passage**

34

Paskey kidnap an author?" asked Ruth Rose. "He sells tons of Wallis Wallace's books!"

"I don't think Mr. Paskey is the kidnapper," Dink said. "But in a way, Josh is right. Detectives should consider everyone a suspect, just the way they do in Wallis Wallace's books."

At River Road, they turned left. Two minutes later, Dink pushed open the door of the Lawrence Taxi Service office. He asked the man behind the counter if one of their drivers had met Flight 3132 at Bradley Airport the previous night.

The man ran his finger down a list on a clipboard. "That would be Maureen Higgins. She's out back eating her lunch," he said, pointing over his shoulder. "Walk straight through."

They cut through the building to a grassy area in back. Through the trees,

Dink could see the Indian River. The sun reflected off the water like bright coins.

A woman was sitting at a picnic table eating a sandwich and filling in a crossword puzzle.

"Excuse me, are you Maureen Higgins?" Dink asked.

The woman shook her head without looking up. "Nope, I'm Marilyn Monroe."

The woman wrote in another letter. Then she looked up. She had the merriest blue eyes Dink had ever seen.

"Yeah, cutie pie, I'm Maureen." She pointed her sandwich at Dink. "And who might you be?"

"I'm Dink Duncan," he said. "These are my friends Josh, Ruth Rose, and Mavis."

"We wondered if you could help us," Ruth Rose said.

Maureen stared at them. "How?"

"Did you pick up a man named Wallis Wallace at the airport last night?" Dink asked.

Maureen squinted one of her blue eyes. "Why do you want to know?"

"Because he's missing!" said Josh.

"Well, I sure ain't got him!" Maureen took a bite out of her sandwich. Mayonnaise oozed onto her fingers.

"I know. I mean, we didn't think you had him," Dink said. "But did you pick him up?"

Maureen nodded, swallowing. "Sure I picked him up. Seven o'clock sharp, I was there with my sign saying WALLACE. The guy spots me, trots over, I take him out to my taxi. He climbs in, carrying a small suitcase. Kinda spooky guy. Dressed in a hat, long raincoat, sunglasses. Sunglasses at night! Doesn't speak a word, just sits. Spooky!"

38

"Did you take him to the Shangri-la Hotel?" Dink asked.

"Yep. Those were my orders. Guy didn't have to give directions, but it woulda been nice if he'd said something. Pass the time, you know? Lotta people, they chat just to act friendly. Not this one. Quiet as a mouse in the back seat."

Maureen wiped mayonnaise from her fingers and lips. "Who is this Wallace fella, anyway?"

"He's a famous writer!" Ruth Rose said.

Maureen's mouth fell open. "You mean I had a celebrity in my cab and never even knew it?"

"What happened when you got to the hotel?" Josh asked.

Maureen stood up and tossed her napkin into the trash. "I get out of my side, then I open his door. He hops out,

hands me a twenty. Last I seen, he's scooting into the lobby."

Dink pulled out the itinerary. He crossed out TAXI with a thick black line. Then he drew a question mark next to HOTEL.

"Thanks a lot, Miss Higgins," he said. "Come on, guys, I have a feeling we're getting closer to finding Wallis Wallace."

Maureen put her hand on Dink's arm. "I just thought of something," she said. "When he handed me my fare, this Wallace fella was smiling."

Dink stared at Maureen. "Smiling?"

She nodded. "Yep. Had a silly grin on his face. Like he knew some big secret or something."

## ENTRY 3

### COMPREHENSION PROCESSES

Understand, Apply, Create

### WRITING TRAITS

Conventions—Complete Sentence,
Capital, Question Mark

**Identifying—What, Who, When**

**Inferring, Describing**

**Identifying—Where**

**Generating Ideas, Asking Questions**

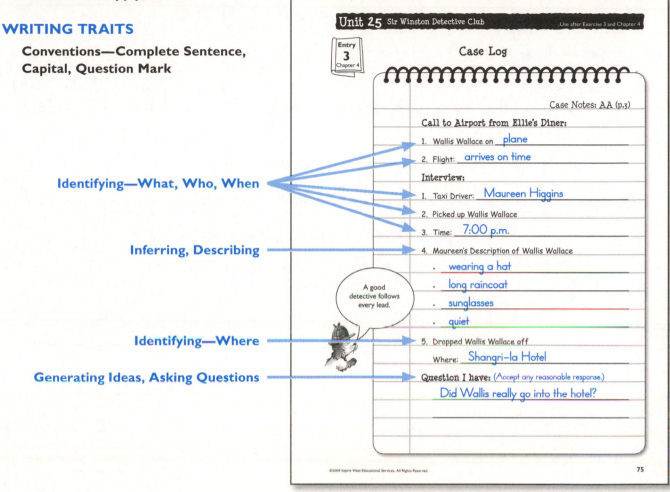

## PROCEDURES

Discuss each step. Then have students complete the page independently.

1. **Note Taking: Summarizing—Basic Instructions** (Items 1, 2, 3, 5)
   Have students read each item and fill in the blanks.

2. **Note Taking: Description—Basic Instructions** (Item 4)
   Have students list four things Maureen said that describe Wallis Wallace.

3. **Note Taking: Asking Questions—Specific Instructions** (Questions I have)
   Have students brainstorm questions they have, then write one question in the blank.
   Remind students to start their question with a capital and end with a question mark.

### VOCABULARY LOG • WORD FAMILY

### COMPREHENSION PROCESSES
**Understand, Apply**

### WRITING TRAITS
**Conventions—Period**

### PROCEDURES
For each step, demonstrate and guide practice, as needed. Then have students complete the page independently.

**Vocabulary: Sentence Completion—Specific Instructions**
- Have students read the vocabulary words and complete the definitions.
- Have students complete the sentences for each vocabulary word. Remind them to end with a period.
- Have students draw a picture in the box to illustrate the sentence.

**Defining and Using Vocabulary— suspicious, suspect, suspicion**

The Absent Author

## Unit 25 Activity 3
Use after Exercise 3 and Chapter 4

Name _____

### Vocabulary Log • Word Family

Related words are a family. If you know the meaning of one word, you can figure out the meaning of a related word.

| Word | Definition | Sentence | Picture |
|------|-----------|----------|---------|
| You know the word:<br><br>**suspicious** | When something is suspicious, you think that something is . . .<br><u>not quite right.</u><br>_____ | Officer Fallon thought that letters from Wallis Wallace were<br><u>suspicious.</u> | |
| Related word:<br><br>**suspect** | A suspect is a person who you think did . . .<br><u>something</u><br><u>suspicious.</u> | Mr. Paskey was nervous, so Josh thought Mr. Paskey was a<br><u>suspect.</u> | |
| Related word:<br><br>**suspicion** | A suspicion is a feeling that someone has . . .<br><u>done something</u><br><u>wrong.</u> | Josh's suspicion was that Mr. Paskey had<br><u>kidnapped Wallis</u><br><u>Wallace.</u> | |

83

### ❶ SOUND REVIEW

### ❷ ACCURACY AND FLUENCY BUILDING

> ┌─────────────────────────┐
> │ **MULTISYLLABIC** │
> │ **WORDS** │
> │ **CORRECTION** │
> │ **PROCEDURE** │
> │ If students make an error, │
> │ put the word on the │
> │ board. Draw loops under │
> │ each syllable and guide │
> │ practice with your hand. │
> │ Have students say each │
> │ syllable then read the │
> │ whole word. │
> └─────────────────────────┘

- For each task, have students say any underlined part, then read the word.
- Set a pace. Then have students read the whole words in each task and column.
- Provide repeated practice, building accuracy first, then fluency.

#### C1. Multisyllabic Words

Have students read each whole word. Use each word in a sentence, as needed.

#### D1. Word Endings

Have students read the underlined word, then the word with an ending. Use the words in sentences, as needed.

#### E1. Tricky Words

- For each Tricky Word, have students use the sounds and word parts they know to silently sound out the word. Use the word in a sentence to help with pronunciation.

**mustache**
Look at the first word. Say the word parts silently. Thumbs up when you know the word. Use my sentence to help you pronounce the word. The man has a beard and a . . . *mustache*. Read the word two times. (mustache, mustache)

| | |
|---|---|
| **answering** | Carmen checked for messages on the . . . *answering* . . . machine. |
| **toward** | The opposite of away from is . . . *toward*. |
| **young** | The opposite of old is . . . *young*. |

- Have students go back and read the whole words in the column.

### ❸ MULTISYLLABIC WORDS

For each word, have students read the syllables, then the whole word. Use the word in a sentence, as appropriate.

| | |
|---|---|
| **immediately** | Mom said, "I want you to clean your room . . . *immediately*." |
| **innocently** | The naughty dog looked at his owner . . . *innocently*. |
| **signature** | May got out her autograph book and asked for the celebrity's . . . *signature*. |
| **relieved** | When Jeff found out his mom had gotten home safely, he was . . . *relieved*. |

### ❹ NAMES AND PLACES

### ❺ MORPHOGRAPHS AND AFFIXES

- Have students read the underlined part, then the whole word.
- Repeat practice with whole words, mixing group and individual turns. Build accuracy, then fluency.

### ❻ GENERALIZATION: READING NEW WORDS IN PARAGRAPHS

- Have students read the paragraph silently, then out loud. Tell students to use the sounds and word parts they know to read any difficult words.
- Repeat practice, as needed.

The Absent Author

# Unit 25 Exercise 4
Use before Chapter 5

1. **SOUND REVIEW** Have students review sounds for accuracy, then for fluency.

| Ⓐ | au | oy | ew | gi | igh |
|---|----|----|----|----|----|
| Ⓑ | aw | u_e | ci | ph | -dge |

**MIX IT UP**
**(Reminder)**

Response forms can be varied. Have students say the sounds using different rhythms. Have students use big voices, small voices, and deep voices. Pass the cards to students. Then have them find and return a sound. Be creative, but maintain a high rate of group responses.

2. **ACCURACY/FLUENCY BUILDING** For each column, have students say any underlined part, then read each word. Next, have them read the column.

| **A1** <br> Mixed Practice | **B1** <br> Compound Words | **C1** <br> Multisyllabic Words | **D1** <br> Word Endings | **E1** <br> Tricky Words |
|---|---|---|---|---|
| smu<u>dge</u>d | lunchbox | preferred | <u>supposed</u> | mustache |
| <u>a</u>ware | airport | register | <u>sa</u>ddest | answering |
| scr<u>aw</u>led | suitcase | excuse | <u>sigh</u>ing | toward |
| sh<u>ow</u>n | | yesterday | <u>approached</u> | young |

3. **MULTISYLLABIC WORDS** Have students read each word part, then read each whole word.

| Ⓐ | im·me·di·ate·ly | immediately | in·no·cent·ly | innocently |
|---|---|---|---|---|
| Ⓑ | sig·na·ture | signature | re·lieved | relieved |

4. **NAMES AND PLACES** Have students use the sounds and word parts they know to figure out the words.

| Maureen Higgins | Mavis Green | Book Nook | Wallis Wallace |
|---|---|---|---|

5. **MORPHOGRAPHS AND AFFIXES** Have students read each underlined part, then the word.

| fam<u>ous</u> | <u>ex</u>plained | foolish<u>ness</u> | replace<u>able</u> |
|---|---|---|---|

6. **GENERALIZATION** Have students read the paragraphs silently, then out loud. (New words: Linkletter, eyebrows, adjusted, madam, droopy)

Mr. Linkletter raised his eyebrows and adjusted his tie. "Madam," he said, "this hotel is full, but the Shangri-la Hotel has a room. Would you like me to call a taxi to take you there? You can wait in the lobby until it arrives."

"Yes, please," said Mrs. Green. As Mr. Linkletter phoned for a cab, he twirled one end of his droopy mustache. Mrs. Green sat down to wait.

## COMPREHENSION PROCESSES

Understand, Apply

## PROCEDURES

### Introducing Vocabulary

★prefer ★relieved ★innocently ★adjust

- For each vocabulary word, have students read the word by parts, then read the whole word.
- Read the student-friendly explanations to students as they follow with their fingers. Then have students use the vocabulary word by following the gray text.
- Review and discuss the illustrations.
  *Note*: Student vocabulary pages for this unit are found in the students' *Exercise Book 4.*

**USING VOCABULARY**

The Absent Author

## Unit 25  Vocabulary 4
Use after Exercise 4

★**pre·fer**

When you **prefer** something, you like it better.

Josh *prefers* apples to oranges. What would Josh rather eat—an apple or an orange?[1]

★**re·lieved**

People who are **relieved** are happy because they no longer have to worry about something.

Jonathan was *relieved* to find his puppy. Why do you think he was relieved?[2]

❶ **Understand:** Using Vocabulary—prefer  (Josh would rather eat an apple.)

❷ **Apply:** Using Vocabulary—relieved  (Jonathan was relieved because he didn't have to worry about his puppy anymore.)

★ = New in this unit

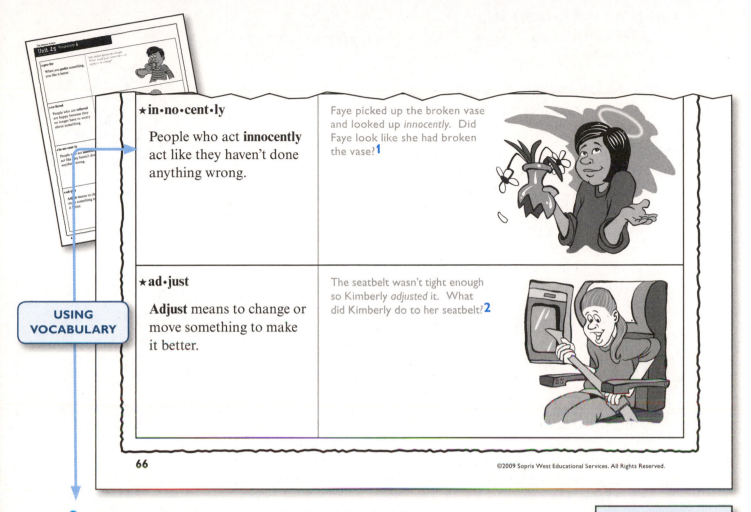

**★in•no•cent•ly**

People who act **innocently** act like they haven't done anything wrong.

Faye picked up the broken vase and looked up *innocently.* Did Faye look like she had broken the vase?**1**

**★ad•just**

**Adjust** means to change or move something to make it better.

The seatbelt wasn't tight enough so Kimberly *adjusted* it. What did Kimberly do to her seatbelt?**2**

**USING VOCABULARY**

66

**❶ Apply:** Using Vocabulary—innocently  (Faye did not look like she had broken the vase.)

**❷ Understand:** Using Vocabulary—adjust  (Kimberly adjusted her seat belt.  She tightened her seatbelt.)

**USING VOCABULARY**

Be enthusiastic about learning new words. Keep a running list of words you would like to use and encourage students to use. Keep the list handy when you are teaching. Put students' names on the board to acknowledge use of a word. Say things like:
Wow! [Amanda] used the word *relieved* to describe how she felt after finding her math homework. That's a great way to use a vocabulary word!

### CHAPTER 5 INSTRUCTIONS

Students read Chapter 5, pages 40–42 with the teacher and pages 43–46 on their own.

### COMPREHENSION PROCESSES

**Remember, Understand, Apply, Analyze**

### PROCEDURES

1. **Reviewing Chapter 4**

   **Summarizing; Describing—Character Traits (Characterization); Predicting**

   Have students turn to page 35. Quickly discuss the questions from the previous Setting a Purpose. Say something like:

   Yesterday, you read pages 35–39 on your own.

   Let's see what you found out.

   How did Maureen Higgins describe Wallace?

   (He was kind of spooky. He wore sunglasses at night. He had on a hat and a long raincoat. He was as quiet as a mouse.)

   Where will Dink and his friends look next?  (They'll go to the hotel.)

2. **Introducing Chapter 5**

   **Using Graphic Organizer—Map**

   Say something like:

   You thought the kids would head to the Shangri-la Hotel next.

   That's the next location on Wallis Wallace's itinerary, and it's where the taxi driver took him.

   Turn to the map. Find the hotel. The Shangri-la Hotel is the setting for the next chapter.

   Turn to Chapter 5 on page 40.

3. **First Reading**

   • Ask questions and discuss the story as indicated by the blue text in this guide.
   • Mix group and individual turns, independent of your voice.
     Have students work toward a group accuracy goal of 0–4 errors.
     Quietly keep track of errors made by all students in the group.
   • After reading the story, practice any difficult words.
     Reread the story if students have not reached the accuracy goal.

4. **Second Reading, Timed Readings: Repeated Reading**

   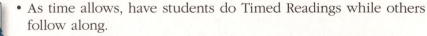
   • As time allows, have students do Timed Readings while others follow along.
   • Time individuals for 30 seconds and encourage each child to work for a personal best.
   • Determine words correct per minute. Record student scores.

Back on Main Street, Dink adjusted his backpack and led the way to the Shangri-la Hotel.

"Maureen Higgins said she dropped him off at the hotel last night," he told the others, "so that's our next stop."

"What if she didn't?" Josh said, catching up to Dink.

"What do you mean?"

"I mean maybe Maureen Higgins wasn't telling the truth. Maybe *she* kidnapped him!"

"And she's hiding him in her lunch-

40

box!" Ruth Rose said.

"Very funny, Ruth Rose," Josh said. "Maureen Higgins said she drove Wallis Wallace to the hotel. But what if she drove him somewhere else?"

"You could be right," Dink said. "That's why we're going to the hotel."

With Dink in the lead, the four approached the check-in counter in the hotel lobby.

"Excuse me," Dink said to the man behind the counter.

"May we help you?" He was the saddest-looking man Dink had ever seen. He had thin black hair and droopy eyebrows. His skinny mustache looked like a sleeping centipede. A name tag on his suit coat said MR. LINKLETTER.

"We're looking for someone."

Mr. Linkletter stared at Dink.

"He's supposed to be staying in this hotel," Josh said.

**After Reading Page 40**

❶ **Remember:** Identifying—Who,
Using Vocabulary—suspect; **Analyze:**
Drawing Conclusions
Who did Josh think was a suspect?
(Josh thought the taxi driver was a suspect.)

❷ Do you think Maureen might have kidnapped
Wallis Wallace? Why or why not?
(Yes, she may be a good suspect. She was the
last to see Wallace. She seems very nice and
cheerful, but it may be an act. We won't know
until we find out if Wallace made it to the hotel.)

42

The man twitched his mustache at Josh.

"His name is Wallis Wallace," Dink explained. "Can you tell us if he checked in last night?"

Mr. Linkletter patted his mustache. "Young sir, if we had such a guest, we wouldn't give out any information. We have *rules* at the Shangri-la," he added in a deep, sad voice.

"But he's missing!" Ruth Rose said. "He was supposed to be at the Book Nook this morning and he never showed up!"

Dink pulled out the itinerary. "See, he was coming here from the airport. The taxi driver said she saw him walk into this lobby."

"And he's famous!" Ruth Rose said. She placed her book on the counter in front of Mr. Linkletter. "He wrote this!"

Sighing, Mr. Linkletter looked down

**Stop Reading Here**

## After Reading Page 42

❶ **Understand:** Explaining
When Mr. Linkletter says "We have *rules* at the Shangri-la," what does he mean?
(Mr. Linkletter means that he's not supposed to give out any information about a guest.)

❷ **Apply:** Inferring, Explaining
Why does Ruth Rose tell Mr. Linkletter that Wallis Wallace is missing and that he's famous?
(Ruth Rose hopes that Mr. Linkletter will bend the rules because Wallis Wallace is famous and might be in trouble.)

## CHAPTER 5 INSTRUCTIONS

Students read Chapter 5, pages 43–46, without the teacher, independently or with partners.

## COMPREHENSION PROCESSES

**Understand, Analyze**

## PROCEDURES FOR READING ON YOUR OWN

**1. Getting Ready**

Have students turn to page 42. Tell them they will start reading at the last line at the bottom of the page.

**2. Setting a Purpose**

**Explaining, Summarizing, Drawing Conclusions**

Before students begin reading, say something like:

As you read the next pages, try to answer these questions:

- What did the kids learn from the hotel register?
- What questions did Dink have at the end of Chapter 5?
- Do you think Wallis Wallace was kidnapped? Why or why not?

**3. Reading on Your Own: Partner or Whisper Reading**

- Have students take turns reading every other page with a partner or have students whisper read pages 43–46 on their own.
- Continue having students track each word with their fingers.

**4. Comprehension and Skill Work**

Tell students they will do Case Log Entry 4 and Comprehension and Skill Activity 4 after they read on their own. Guide practice, as needed. For teacher directions, see pages 74 and 75.

**5. Homework 4: New Passage**

> **PREP NOTE**
>
> **Setting a Purpose**
>
> Write questions on a chalkboard, white board, or large piece of paper before working with your small group.

at Ruth Rose. "We are quite aware of who Mr. Wallace is, young miss."

Mr. Linkletter turned his sad eyes back on Dink. He flipped through the hotel register, glanced at it, then quickly shut the book. "Yes, Mr. Wallace checked in," he said. "He arrived at 8:05."

"He did? What happened after that?" Dink asked.

Mr. Linkletter pointed toward a bank of elevators. "He went to his room. We offered to have his suitcase carried, but he preferred to do it himself."

"Have you seen Mr. Wallace yet today?" Mavis asked.

"No, madam, I haven't seen him. Mr. Wallace is still in his room."

Still in his room!

Suddenly Dink felt relieved. He felt a little foolish, too. Wallis Wallace

44

hadn't been kidnapped after all. He was probably in his room right now!

"Can you call him?" Dink asked.

Mr. Linkletter tapped his fingers on the closed hotel register. He patted his mustache and squinted his eyes at Dink.

"Please?" Dink said. "We just want to make sure he's okay."

Finally Mr. Linkletter turned around. He stepped a few feet away and picked up a red telephone.

As soon as his back was turned, Josh grabbed the hotel register. He quickly found yesterday's page. Dink and the others crowded around Josh for a peek.

Dink immediately recognized Wallis Wallace's signature, scrawled in big loopy letters. He had checked in to Room 303 at five after eight last night.

Dink pulled out his letter from Wallis Wallace and compared the two

signatures. They were exactly the same.

Josh dug his elbow into Dink's side. "Look!" he whispered.

Josh was pointing at the next line in the register. ROOM 302 had been printed there. Check-in time was 8:15.

"Someone else checked in right after

*46*

Wallis Wallace!" Ruth Rose whispered.

"But the signature is all smudged," Dink said. "I can't read the name."

When Mr. Linkletter hung up the phone, Josh shoved the register away.

As Mr. Linkletter turned back around, Dink shut the register. He looked up innocently. "Is he in his room?" Dink asked.

"I don't know." Mr. Linkletter tapped his fingers on his mustache. "There was no answer."

Dink's stomach dropped. His mind raced.

If Wallis Wallace had checked into his room last night, why hadn't he shown up at the Book Nook today?

And why wasn't he answering his phone?

*Maybe Wallis Wallace had been kidnapped after all!*

## ENTRY 4

### COMPREHENSION PROCESSES

Understand, Analyze

### WRITING TRAITS

Conventions—Capital, Period

Identifying—What, Who, Where, When; Drawing Conclusions Sentence Completion

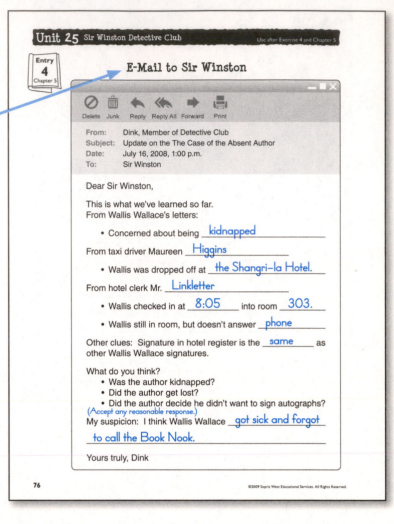

**Unit 25** Sir Winston Detective Club     Use after Exercise 4 and Chapter 5

Entry 4 Chapter 5

## E-Mail to Sir Winston

Delete   Junk   Reply   Reply All   Forward   Print

From:   Dink, Member of Detective Club
Subject:   Update on the The Case of the Absent Author
Date:   July 16, 2008, 1:00 p.m.
To:   Sir Winston

Dear Sir Winston,

This is what we've learned so far.
From Wallis Wallace's letters:

- Concerned about being ___kidnapped___

From taxi driver Maureen ___Higgins___

- Wallis was dropped off at ___the Shangri-la Hotel.___

From hotel clerk Mr. ___Linkletter___

- Wallis checked in at ___8:05___ into room ___303.___
- Wallis still in room, but doesn't answer ___phone___

Other clues: Signature in hotel register is the ___same___ as other Wallis Wallace signatures.

What do you think?
- Was the author kidnapped?
- Did the author get lost?
- Did the author decide he didn't want to sign autographs?

(Accept any reasonable response.)
My suspicion: I think Wallis Wallace ___got sick and forgot to call the Book Nook.___

Yours truly, Dink

76     ©2009 Sopris West Educational Services. All Rights Reserved.

### PROCEDURES

Discuss each step. Then have students complete the page independently.

**Note Taking: Summarizing—Basic Instructions**
Have students read the letter and fill in the blanks. Remind students to use capitals for proper names and to put a period at the end of sentences.

## ADJECTIVES AND ALPHABETICAL ORDER

## COMPREHENSION PROCESSES

Understand, Create

## WRITING TRAITS

Conventions—Capital

**Alphabetical Order, Generating Ideas**

The Absent Author

### Unit 25 Activity 4
Use after Exercise 4 and Chapter 5

Name _____

## Adjectives and Alphabetical Order

1. Fill in the missing letters of the alphabet.
2. Make up the titles of your own A to Z Mysteries. The titles for A, C, I, K, Q, R, T, and Y are done for you. Each word of the title must begin with the same letter. (Accept any reasonable response.)

|   | Adjective | Noun • Person, Place or Thing |
|---|-----------|-------------------------------|
| A | Ancient | Arachnid |
| B | Brilliant | Bat |
| C | Curious | Carnivore |
| D | Discouraged | Dinosaur |
| E | Educated | Elephant |
| F | Frantic | Frog |
| G | Gloomy | Ghost |
| H | Harsh | House |
| I | Invisible | Inventor |
| J | Jealous | Jaguar |
| K | Kind | Kangaroo |
| L | Luscious | Lollipop |
| M | Moody | Monkey |
| N | Nocturnal | Neighbors |
| O | Ordinary | Orangutan |
| P | Popular | Police Officer |
| Q | Quiet | Queen |
| R | Rude | Relative |
| S | Suspicious | Student |
| T | Terrible | Trickster |
| U | Unsettled | Umbrella |
| V | Vast | Vegetable |
| W | Wealthy | Woman |
| XYZ | Yellow | Yarn |

## PROCEDURES

For each step, demonstrate and guide practice, as needed. Then have students complete the page independently.

### 1. Alphabetical Order—Basic Instructions

Have students read the letters in the alphabet column and fill in the missing letters.

### ★ 2. Creating Titles—Specific Instructions

- Have students read the directions and the title in the first row, which is done for them.
- Have students read the adjective in the second row and brainstorm ideas for a noun with the same letter (b) to go with the adjective. Have students write their favorite idea in the blank. Remind them that titles start with capitals.
- Have students complete the remaining titles.

★ = New in this unit

## ❶ SOUND REVIEW
Use selected Sound Cards from Units 1–19.

## ❷ SHIFTY WORDS
Have students read the words. Use the words in sentences, as needed.

## ❸ ACCURACY AND FLUENCY BUILDING
- For each task, have students say any underlined part, then read the word.
- Set a pace. Then have students read the whole words in each task and column.
- Provide repeated practice, building accuracy first, then fluency.

### C1. Multisyllabic Words
- For the list of words divided by syllables, have students read each syllable, then the whole word. Use the word in a sentence, as appropriate.
- For the list of whole words, build accuracy and then fluency.

| | |
|---|---|
| **devours** | Emma loves books. She . . . *devours* . . . them. |
| **scribbled** | I couldn't read Megan's answers because she . . . *scribbled* . . . them. |
| **peckish** | Another word for hungry is . . . *peckish.* |
| **revolving** | The only way to get into the hotel is through its huge . . . *revolving* . . . doors. |
| **stroller** | Even though my little sister is four, she likes to ride in a baby . . . *stroller.* |
| **disturbed** | The fight upset him. He was . . . *disturbed* . . . by it. |
| **interrupt** | Let me finish speaking. Please don't . . . *interrupt.* |

### D2. Rhyming Words
Have students read the words and identify what's the same about them.

## ❹ WORD ENDINGS
Have students read the underlined word, then the word with an ending. Use the words in sentences, as needed.

## ❺ NAMES AND PLACES
- Tell students these are people and places they will be reading about in the story.
- Have students use the sounds and word parts they know to figure out the words. Use the words in sentences, as needed.

## ❻ MORPHOGRAPHS AND AFFIXES
- Have students read the underlined part, then the whole word.
- Repeat practice with whole words, mixing group and individual turns. Build accuracy, then fluency.

## ❼ GENERALIZATION: READING NEW WORDS IN PARAGRAPHS
- Have students read the paragraph silently, then out loud. Tell students to use the sounds and word parts they know to read any difficult words.
- Repeat practice, as needed.

> **SHIFTY WORDS CORRECTION PROCEDURE**
> **(Reminder)**
>
> If students make an error, put the word on the board. Underline the incorrect sound.
>
> Have students identify the difficult sound, then sound the word out smoothly. Have students read the row again. Return to the difficult word for three correct responses.

The Absent Author

# Unit 25 Exercise 5
Use before Chapter 6

1. **SOUND REVIEW**  Use selected Sound Cards from Units 1–19.

2. **SHIFTY WORDS**  Have students read the words.

| brown | crown | clown | clean | clear |
|-------|-------|-------|-------|-------|

3. **ACCURACY/FLUENCY BUILDING**  For each column, have students say any underlined part, then read each word. Next, have them read the column.

| A1 Mixed Practice | B1 Contractions | C1 Multisyllabic Words | | D1 Compound Words |
|-------|-------|-------|-------|-------|
| crime | what did | de•vours | devours | bulldozer |
| piece | what'd | scrib•bled | scribbled | babysitter |
| geez | | peck•ish | peckish | overheard |
| peered | we would | re•volv•ing | revolving | **D2** Rhyming Words |
| fishy | we'd | strol•ler | stroller | lunches |
| | | dis•turbed | disturbed | bunches |
| | | in•ter•rupt | interrupt | munches |

4. **WORD ENDINGS**  Have students read each underlined word, then the word with an ending.

| shifted | muttered | towels | confused |
|-------|-------|-------|-------|

5. **NAMES AND PLACES**  Have students use the sounds and word parts they know to figure out the words.

| Olivia Nugent | Acorn Apartments | Green Lawn Gazette |
|-------|-------|-------|

6. **MORPHOGRAPHS AND AFFIXES**  Have students read each underlined part, then the word.

| firmly | interruption | author | mysterious |
|-------|-------|-------|-------|

7. **GENERALIZATION**  Have students read the paragraph silently, then out loud.  (New words: maid, ghost, doorknob)

As the maid walked into the hotel room, she thought she saw a shadowy figure around the corner.  "Oh my goodness," she thought, "a ghost!"  She dropped her sandwich and tried to run out of the room, but she couldn't twist the doorknob.  It was stuck.  Just as she was about to panic, she realized she was seeing the picture of a New York baseball player hanging on the wall.

67

## COMPREHENSION PROCESSES

**Understand, Apply**

## PROCEDURES

**Introducing Vocabulary**

> ★ **disturb**  ★ **smells fishy**  ★ **devour, imitate**

- For each vocabulary word, have students read the word by parts, then read the whole word.
- Read the student-friendly explanations to students as they follow with their fingers. Then have students use the vocabulary word by following the gray text.
- Review and discuss the illustrations.
  *Note*: Student vocabulary pages for this unit are found in the students' *Exercise Book 4*.

The Absent Author

# Unit 25 Vocabulary 5
Use after Exercise 5

**USING VOCABULARY**

★ **dis•turb**

**Disturb** means to interrupt someone.

The kids wanted to finish their map. They didn't want to be *disturbed*.

What's another way to say the kids didn't want to be interrupted?**1**

★ **smells fish•y**

When something **smells fishy**, it may not be the truth.

His story about finding the dinosaur bone *smells fishy*.

What kind of story could it be?**2**

**1** **Apply:** Using Vocabulary—disturb (The kids didn't want to be disturbed.)

**2** **Apply:** Using Idioms and Expressions—smells fishy (The story could be made up. It may not be the truth.)

★ = New in this unit

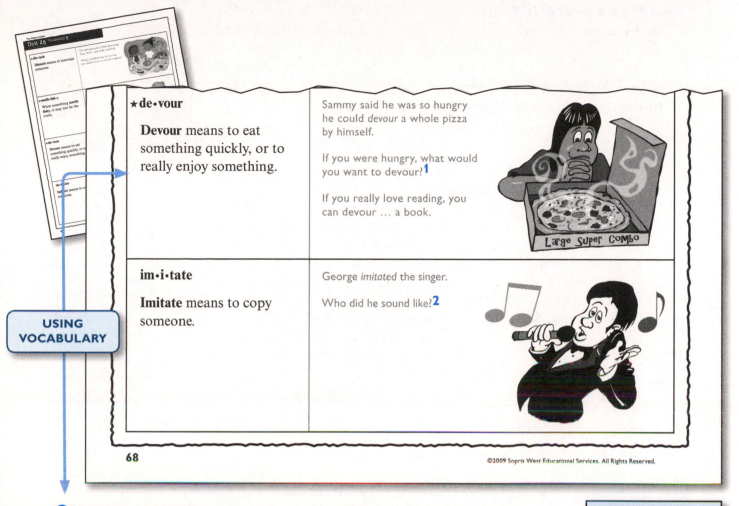

**USING VOCABULARY**

★ de•vour

**Devour** means to eat something quickly, or to really enjoy something.

Sammy said he was so hungry he could *devour* a whole pizza by himself.

If you were hungry, what would you want to devour?**1**

If you really love reading, you can devour ... a book.

Large Super Combo

im•i•tate

**Imitate** means to copy someone.

George *imitated* the singer.

Who did he sound like?**2**

68

**1 Understand:** Using Vocabulary—devour  (If I were hungry, I'd want to devour some [hamburgers].)

**2 Apply:** Using Vocabulary—imitate  (George sounded like the singer.)

**USING VOCABULARY**

Be enthusiastic about learning new words. Keep a running list of words you would like to use and encourage students to use. Keep the list handy when you are teaching. Put students' names on the board to acknowledge use of a word. Say things like:

Wow! [Jeff] used the word *devour* when he told us about his lunch. What a great way to use a vocabulary word!

### CHAPTER 6 INSTRUCTIONS

Students read Chapter 6, pages 47–50 with the teacher and pages 51–55 on their own.

### COMPREHENSION PROCESSES

**Remember, Understand, Apply, Analyze**

### PROCEDURES

1. **Reviewing Chapter 5**

   **Summarizing, Drawing Conclusions**
   Quickly review what has happened in the story so far. Discuss the questions from the previous Setting a Purpose. Say something like:
   Yesterday you read pages 43–46 on your own. Let's see what you found out.
   What did the kids learn from the hotel register?
   (Wallis Wallace checked in at 8:05 and went to Room 303. Someone else checked into Room 302 at 8:15.)
   What questions did Dink have at the end of the chapter?
   (Why didn't Wallace shown up at the Book Nook if he checked into the hotel? Why wasn't he answering his phone? Had Wallace been kidnapped?)
   Do you think Wallis Wallace was kidnapped?
   (Yes, no one knows where he is. No, he could be sleeping in his room.)

   > **REPEATED READINGS**
   > **Prosody**
   > On the second reading, students practice developing prosody—phrasing and expression. Research has shown that prosody is related to both fluency and comprehension.

2. **Introducing Chapter 6**

   **Defining and Using Vocabulary—suspense; Predicting**
   Say something like:
   The author left us in suspense at the end of the last chapter.
   What does that mean? (He left us wondering what will happen next.)
   What do you think might happen next?

3. **First Reading**
   - Ask questions and discuss the text as indicated by the blue text in this guide.
   - Mix group and individual turns, independent of your voice.
     Have students work toward a group accuracy goal of 0–6 errors.
     Quietly keep track of errors made by all students in the group.
   - After reading the story, practice any difficult words.
     Repeat, if students have not reached the accuracy goal.

4. **Second Reading, Short Passage Practice: Developing Prosody**
   - Demonstrate expressive, fluent reading of the first paragraph. Read at a rate slightly faster than the students' rate.
   - Guide practice with your voice.
   - Provide individual turns while others track with their fingers and whisper read.
   - Repeat with one paragraph at a time.

Dink stared at Mr. Linkletter. "No answer? Are you sure?"

Mr. Linkletter nodded. He looked puzzled. "Perhaps he's resting and doesn't want to be disturbed."

"Can we go up and see?" Ruth Rose smiled sweetly at Mr. Linkletter. "Then we'd know for sure."

Mr. Linkletter shook his head. "We cannot disturb our guests, young miss. We have *rules* at the Shangri-la. Now good day, and thank you."

47

48

Ruth Rose opened her mouth. "But, Mis—"

"Good day," Mr. Linkletter said firmly again.

Dink and the others walked toward the door.

"Something smells fishy," muttered Dink.

"Yeah," Josh said, "and I think it's that Linkletter guy. See how he tried to hide the register? Then he turned his back. Maybe he didn't even call Room 303. Maybe he was warning his partners in crime!"

"What are you suggesting, Josh?" Mavis asked.

"Maybe Mr. Linkletter is the kidnapper," Josh said. "He was the last one to see Wallis Wallace."

A man wearing a red cap tapped Dink on the shoulder. "Excuse me, but I overheard you talking to my boss, Mr.

## After Reading Pages 47 and 48

**❶ Apply:** Inferring, Explaining, Using Idioms and Expressions—smells fishy
Why did Dink think something smelled fishy?
(Mr. Linkletter was trying to get the kids to leave. He kept saying, "Good day.")

**❷ Understand:** Explaining, Using Vocabulary—suspect
Why does Josh think Mr. Linkletter might be a suspect in the kidnapping?
(Mr. Linkletter tried to hide the register. He was the last one to see Wallis Wallace. He won't bend the rules and let the kids go up to Wallace's room.)

Linkletter. Maybe I can help you find Wallis Wallace. My kids love his books."

"Great!" Dink said. "Can you get us into his room?"

The man shook his head. "No, but I know the maid who cleaned the third-floor rooms this morning. Maybe she noticed something."

With his back to Mr. Linkletter, the man scribbled a few words on a pad and handed the page to Dink. "Good luck!" the man whispered, and hurried away.

"What'd he write?" Josh asked.

"Outside," Dink said.

They all shoved through the revolving door. In front of the hotel, Dink looked at the piece of paper. "The maid's name is Olivia Nugent. She lives at the Acorn Apartments, Number Four."

---

50

"Livvy Nugent? I know her!" Ruth Rose said. "She used to be my baby-sitter."

"The Acorn is right around the corner on Oak Street," Dink said. "Let's go!"

Soon all four were standing in front of Livvy Nugent's door. She answered it with a baby in her arms. Another little kid held on to her leg and stared at Dink and the others. He had peanut butter all over his face and in his hair.

"Hi," the boy's mother said. "I'm not buying any cookies and I already get the *Green Lawn Gazette*." She was wearing a man's blue shirt and jeans. Her brown hair stuck out from under a Yankees baseball cap.

"Livvy, it's me!" Ruth Rose said.

Olivia stared at Ruth Rose, then broke into a grin.

"Ruth Rose, you're so big! What are

**Stop Reading Here** ←

---

## After Reading Pages 49 and 50

**❶ Understand:** Explaining
Why did the kids want to find Olivia Nugent?
(Olivia Nugent was the maid who cleaned the third-floor rooms. They hoped she could give them some clues about Wallis Wallace.)

**❷ Understand:** Explaining
How did Ruth Rose know Olivia Nugent?
(Olivia Nugent used to be Ruth Rose's babysitter.)

**❸ Apply:** Inferring, Explaining
At first, what did Olivia Nugent think the kids wanted?
(She thought they were selling cookies or newspaper subscriptions.)

## CHAPTER 6 INSTRUCTIONS

Students read Chapter 6, pages 51–55, without the teacher, independently or with partners.

## COMPREHENSION PROCESSES

**Understand, Apply, Analyze**

## PROCEDURES FOR READING ON YOUR OWN

**1. Getting Ready**

Have students turn to page 50. Tell them they will start reading at the last line at the bottom of the page.

**2. Setting a Purpose**

**Summarizing, Predicting, Drawing Conclusions**

Before students begin reading, say something like:

Read to find out the answers to these questions:
- What clues did Olivia provide?
- What will Dink and his friends do next?
- Where do you think Wallis Wallace is?

> **PREP NOTE**
> **Setting a Purpose**
> Write questions on a chalkboard, white board, or large piece of paper before working with your small group.

**3. Reading on Your Own: Partner or Whisper Reading**
- Have students take turns reading every other page with a partner or have students whisper read pages 51–55 on their own.
- Continue having students track each word with their fingers.

**4. Comprehension and Skill Work**

Tell students they will do Case Log Entry 5 and Comprehension and Skill Activity 5 after they read on their own. Guide practice, as needed. For teacher directions, see pages 87 and 88.)

**5. Homework 5: New Passage**

you up to these days?"

"A man at the hotel gave us your name."

"What man?"

"He was sort of old, wearing a red cap," Dink said.

Livvy chuckled. "Freddy old? He's only thirty! So why did he send you to see me?"

"He told us you cleaned the rooms on the third floor this morning," Dink said. "Did you clean Room 303?"

Livvy Nugent shifted the baby to her other arm. "Randy, please stop pulling on Mommy's leg. Why don't you go finish your lunch?" Randy ran back into the apartment.

"No," Livvy told Dink. "Nobody slept in that room. The bed was still made this morning. The towels were still clean and dry. I remember because there were two rooms in a row that I

didn't have to clean—303 and 302. Room 302 had a Do Not Disturb sign hanging on the doorknob. So I came home early, paid off the baby-sitter, and made our lunches."

"But Mr. Linkletter told us Wallis Wallace checked into Room 303 last night," Ruth Rose said.

"Not *the* Wallis Wallace? The mystery writer? My kid sister *devours* his books!"

Dink nodded. "He was supposed to sign books at the Book Nook this morning. But he never showed up!"

"We even saw his signature on the hotel register," Ruth Rose said.

"Well, Wallis Wallace might have signed in, but he never slept in that room." Livvy grinned. "Unless he's a ghost."

"I wonder if Mr. Linkletter could have made a mistake about the room number," Mavis suggested quietly.

Livvy smiled at Mavis. "You must not be from around here. Mr. Linkletter *never* makes mistakes."

"So Wallis Wallace signed in, but he didn't sleep in his room," said Dink.

54

"That means..."

"Someone must have kidnapped him before he went to bed!" Josh said.

Livvy's eyes bugged. "Kidnapped! Geez, Mr. Linkletter will have a fit." She imitated his voice. "We have *rules* about kidnappings at the Shangri-la!"

Everyone except Dink laughed. All he could think about was Wallis Wallace, his favorite author, kidnapped.

Suddenly a crash came from inside the apartment. "Oops, gotta run," Livvy said. "Randy is playing bulldozer with his baby sister's stroller again. I hope you find Wallis Wallace. My kid sister will die if he doesn't write another book!"

They walked slowly back to Main Street. Dink felt as though his brain was spinning around inside his head.

Now he felt certain that Wallis Wallace had been kidnapped.

But who did it? And when?

*And where was Wallis Wallace being kept?*

"Guys, I'm feeling confused," he said. "Can we just sit somewhere and go over the facts again?"

"Good idea," Josh said. "I always think better when I'm eating."

"I'm feeling a bit peckish, too," Mavis said. "I need a quiet cup of tea and a sandwich. Should we meet again after lunch?"

Ruth Rose looked at her watch. "Let's meet at two o'clock."

"Where?" Josh asked.

"Back at the hotel." Dink peered through the door glass at Mr. Linkletter.

"Unless Maureen Higgins and Mr. Linkletter are *both* lying," he said, "Wallis Wallace walked into the Shangri-la last night—and never came out."

## ENTRY 5

### COMPREHENSION PROCESSES

Understand, Analyze

### WRITING TRAITS

Conventions—Capital, Period

**Identifying—What, Who, Where
Drawing Conclusions
Sentence Completion**

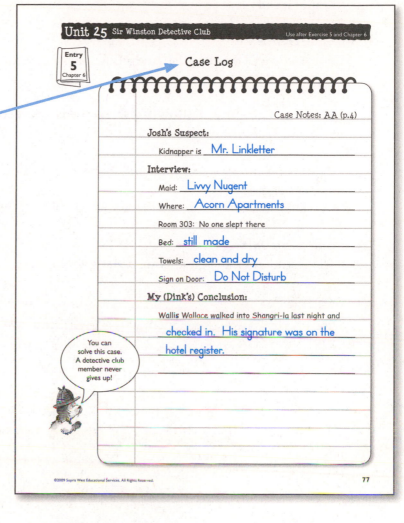

Unit 25 Sir Winston Detective Club — Use after Exercise 5 and Chapter 6

Entry 5 Chapter 6

Case Log

Case Notes: AA (p.4)

Josh's Suspect:

Kidnapper is  Mr. Linkletter

Interview:

Maid:  Livvy Nugent

Where:  Acorn Apartments

Room 303: No one slept there

Bed:  still made

Towels:  clean and dry

Sign on Door:  Do Not Disturb

My (Dink's) Conclusion:

Wallis Wallace walked into Shangri-la last night and checked in.  His signature was on the hotel register.

You can solve this case. A detective club member never gives up!

©2009 Sopris West Educational Services. All Rights Reserved.    77

## PROCEDURES

Discuss each step. Then have students complete the page independently.

**Note Taking: Summarizing—Basic Instructions**

Have students read the case notes and fill in the blanks. Remind students to use capitals for proper names and to put a period at the end of sentences.

## STORY COMPREHENSION • FOLLOWING DIRECTIONS

### COMPREHENSION PROCESSES

**Understand**

### PROCEDURES

For each step, demonstrate and guide practice, as needed. Then have students complete the page independently.

1. **Map: Labeling, Following Directions—Specific Instructions** (Items 1, 2, 5)
   Have students read and follow the directions.

2. **Map: Sentence Completion, Labeling, Following Directions—Specific Instructions** (Items 3, 4)
   Have students fill in the blanks to complete the sentences, then label the map as directed.

*Self-monitoring*

Have students check and correct their work.

**Using Graphic Organizer Identifying— What, Where Sentence Completion**

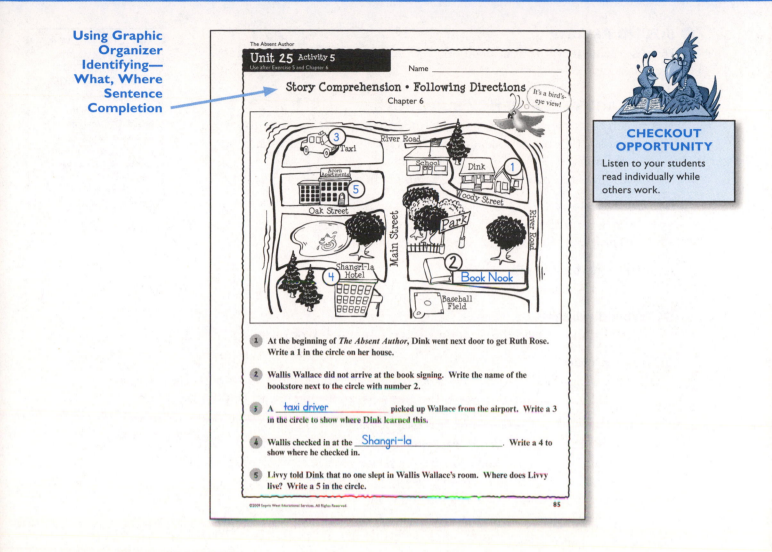

The Absent Author

**Unit 25** Activity 5
Use after Exercise 5 and Chapter 6

Name _____

## Story Comprehension • Following Directions
### Chapter 6

*It's a bird's-eye view!*

1. At the beginning of *The Absent Author*, Dink went next door to get Ruth Rose. Write a 1 in the circle on her house.

2. Wallis Wallace did not arrive at the book signing. Write the name of the bookstore next to the circle with number 2.

3. A ___taxi driver___ picked up Wallace from the airport. Write a 3 in the circle to show where Dink learned this.

4. Wallis checked in at the ___Shangri-la___. Write a 4 to show where he checked in.

5. Livvy told Dink that no one slept in Wallis Wallace's room. Where does Livvy live? Write a 5 in the circle.

85

**CHECKOUT OPPORTUNITY**

Listen to your students read individually while others work.

**①  SOUND REVIEW**

Have students read the sounds and key word phrases. Work for accuracy, then fluency.

**②  ACCURACY AND FLUENCY BUILDING**

- For each task, have students say any underlined part, then read the word.
- Set a pace. Then have students read the whole words in each task and column.
- Provide repeated practice, building accuracy first, then fluency.

> **MULTISYLLABIC WORDS CORRECTION PROCEDURE**
>
> If students make an error, put the word on the board. Draw loops under each syllable and guide practice with your hand. Have students say each syllable then read the whole word.

**B1. Contractions**

- Prompt students to tell you what a contraction is.
- Have students read the words, then the contraction.

**C1. Multisyllabic Words**

Have students read each whole word. Use each word in a sentence, as needed.

**D1. Word Endings**

Have students read the underlined word, then the word with an ending.

**E1.  Tricky Words**

- For each Tricky Word, have students use the sounds and word parts they know to silently sound out the word. Use the word in a sentence to help with pronunciation.

| | |
|---|---|
| **weird** | His hairdo was peculiar. It was . . . *weird.* |
| **signing** | The author was looking forward to meeting people at his book . . . *signing.* |
| **brought** | My friend had a birthday. Everyone . . . *brought* . . . presents. |
| **laughed** | Tia said, "If the joke was funny, I would have . . . *laughed.*" |
| **busy** | Kim is doing a lot. She is very . . . *busy.* |

- Have students go back and read the whole words in the column.

**③  MULTISYLLABIC WORDS**

For each word, have students read the syllables, then the whole word. Use the word in a sentence, as appropriate.

| | |
|---|---|
| **satisfied** | Jake was happy with his birthday presents. He was . . . *satisfied.* |
| **victim** | The woman had her purse stolen. She was a crime . . . *victim.* |
| **preserve** | We want to save our park from being destroyed. We want to . . . *preserve* . . . it. |
| **stupidly** | Cindy didn't know what to do, so she just grinned . . . *stupidly.* |
| **interrupted** | Pete couldn't get his project done because he was . . . *interrupted.* |
| **kidnapping** | The people were guilty of . . . *kidnapping.* |

**④  NAMES AND PLACES**

- Tell students these are people and places they will be reading about in the story.
- Have students use the sounds and word parts they know to figure out the words. Use the words in sentences, as needed.

**⑤  MORPHOGRAPHS AND AFFIXES**

- Have students read the underlined part, then the whole word.
- Repeat practice with whole words, mixing group and individual turns. Build accuracy, then fluency.

## ❻ GENERALIZATION: READING NEW WORDS IN PARAGRAPHS

- Have students read the paragraph silently, then out loud. Tell students to use the sounds and word parts they know to read any difficult words.
- Repeat practice, as needed.

---

The Absent Author

## Unit 25 Exercise 6
Use before Chapter 7

**1. SOUND REVIEW** Have students review sounds for accuracy, then for fluency.

| Ⓐ | ea as in bread | ow as in snow | o as in open | oa as in boat | i as in silence |
|---|---|---|---|---|---|
| Ⓑ | aw | ue | kn | oi | ce |

**2. ACCURACY/FLUENCY BUILDING** For each column, have students say any underlined part, then read each word. Next, have them read the column.

| A1<br>Mixed Practice | B1<br>Contractions | C1<br>Multisyllabic Words | D1<br>Word Endings | E1<br>Tricky Words |
|---|---|---|---|---|
| y<u>ow</u>l | what are | signature | b<u>ugg</u>ing | weird |
| resc<u>ue</u> | what're | waggled | m<u>unch</u>ing | signing |
| <u>kn</u>ocked | who had | naturally | bl<u>ott</u>ed | brought |
| lobby | who'd | liquid | sp<u>ill</u>ed | laughed |
| <u>au</u>thor | | | <u>cl</u>ues | busy |
| | there is | | | |
| | there's | | | |

**3. MULTISYLLABIC WORDS** Have students read each word part, then read each whole word.

| Ⓐ | sat•is•fied | satisfied | vic•tim | victim |
|---|---|---|---|---|
| Ⓑ | pre•serve | preserve | stu•pid•ly | stupidly |
| Ⓒ | in•ter•rupt•ed | interrupted | kid•nap•ping | kidnapping |

**4. NAMES AND PLACES** Have students use the sounds and word parts they know to figure out the words.

| Moose Manor | Ellie's Diner | Olivia Nugent |
|---|---|---|

**5. MORPHOGRAPHS AND AFFIXES** Have students read the underlined word part, then the word.

| hand<u>ful</u> | thoughtful<u>ly</u> | <u>dis</u>cover | <u>re</u>opened |
|---|---|---|---|

**6. GENERALIZATION** Have students read the paragraph silently, then out loud. (New words: headache, tuna, raisins, lemonade)

Livvy was getting ready to go out to dinner with Duncan. Then he called to say he had a terrible headache and couldn't make it. "Now what will I eat?" thought Livvy. She rummaged in the cupboards and found a can of tuna and some raisins. "That'll do," she thought. "Now I'll just make a sandwich and some lemonade."

69

> **ENTHUSIASM**
>
> Make a special effort to acknowledge what students can do.
>
> Say things like: You can read multisyllabic words without help from adults.
>
> You can figure out words you've never seen before.
>
> You can read and use snazzy words like: *satisfied, preserve,* and *interrupted . . .* That is very impressive.

## COMPREHENSION PROCESSES

**Understand, Apply**

## PROCEDURES

**Introducing Vocabulary**

> ★ **preserve** ★ **satisfied, inspiration**

- For each vocabulary word, have students read the word by parts, then read the whole word.
- Read the student-friendly explanations to students as they follow with their fingers. Then have students use the vocabulary word by following the gray text.
- Review and discuss the photos and illustrations.

  *Note*: Student vocabulary pages for this unit are found in the students' *Exercise Book 4*.

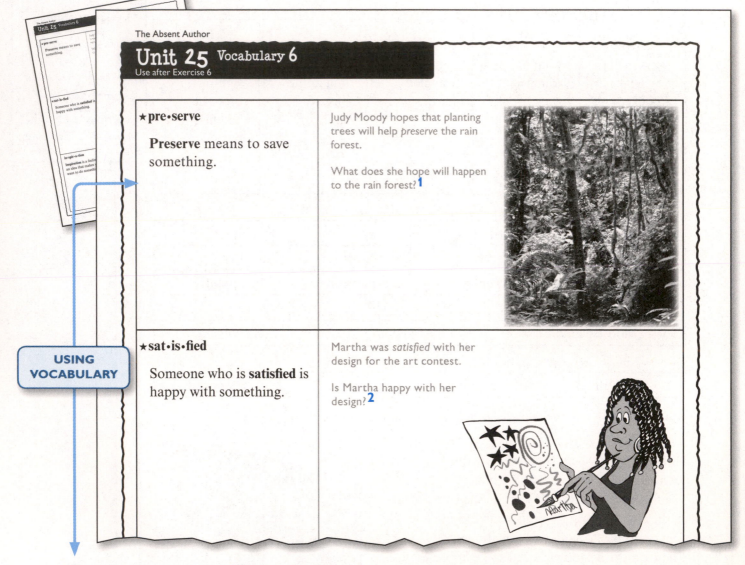

The Absent Author

# Unit 25 Vocabulary 6
Use after Exercise 6

**USING VOCABULARY**

★ **pre•serve**

**Preserve** means to save something.

Judy Moody hopes that planting trees will help *preserve* the rain forest.

What does she hope will happen to the rain forest? **1**

★ **sat•is•fied**

Someone who is **satisfied** is happy with something.

Martha was *satisfied* with her design for the art contest.

Is Martha happy with her design? **2**

❶ **Apply:** Using Vocabulary—preserve  (She hopes the rain forest will be saved.)

❷ **Understand:** Using Vocabulary—satisfied  (Yes, Martha is happy with her design.)

★ = New in this unit

in•spir•a•tion

**Inspiration** is a feeling or an idea that makes you want to do something.

Watching the movie about hiking in the mountains looked wonderful. It gave me *inspiration*.

What do you think I did the next day?[1]

**USING VOCABULARY**

70

❶ **Apply:** Using Vocabulary—inspiration  (You probably went hiking.)

### USING VOCABULARY

Be enthusiastic about learning new words. Keep a running list of words you would like to use and encourage students to use. Keep the list handy when you are teaching. Put students' names on the board to acknowledge use of a word. Say things like:
Wow! [Adam] used the word *satisfied* when he saw his grade for the spelling test. That's a great way to use a vocabulary word!

### CHAPTER 7 INSTRUCTIONS

Students read Chapter 7, pages 56–60 with the teacher and pages 61–65 on their own.

### COMPREHENSION PROCESSES

**Remember, Understand, Apply, Analyze, Create**

### PROCEDURES

**1. Reviewing Chapter 6**
**Summarizing; Predicting; Drawing Conclusions;**
**Using Vocabulary—review**

Have students turn to page 51. Quickly discuss the questions from the previous Setting a Purpose. Say something like:

Yesterday, you read pages 51–55 on your own. Let's see what you found out.
What clues did Olivia provide?

(No one slept in Wallis' room last night.  The bed was made and the towels were dry.  The room next door had a "Do Not Disturb" sign on the door.)

What will Dink and his friends do next?

(They will sit down and review the facts.  They will eat lunch.)

Where do you think Wallis Wallace is?  (The kidnappers have him . . . )

**2. Introducing Chapter 7, pages 56–60**

**Generating Ideas**

Say something like:

I wonder what happened to Wallis Wallace.

Maybe we can figure it out when the kids review their clues.

What do you think they need to find out next?

(They need to find out why Wallace didn't sleep in his room.  They need to find out what happened to him at the hotel . . . )

**3. First Reading**

- Ask questions and discuss the story as indicated by the blue text in this guide.
- Mix group and individual turns, independent of your voice.
  Have students work toward a group accuracy goal of 0–5 errors.
  Quietly keep track of errors made by all students in the group.
- After reading the story, practice any difficult words.
  Reread the story if students have not reached the accuracy goal.

**4. Second Reading, Timed Readings: Repeated Reading**

- As time allows, have students do Timed Readings while others follow along.
- Time individuals for 30 seconds and encourage each child to work for a personal best.
- Determine words correct per minute. Record student scores.

**Chapter 7**

Dink, Josh, and Ruth Rose left Mavis at Ellie's Diner, then headed for Dink's house. Dink made tuna sandwiches and lemonade. Ruth Rose brought a bag of potato chips and some raisin cookies from her house next door.

They ate at the picnic table in Dink's backyard. Dink took a bite of his sandwich. After he swallowed, he said, "Let's go over what we know."

He moved his lemonade glass to the middle of the table. "My glass is the air-

56

port," he said. "We know Wallis Wallace landed."

"How do we *know* he did?" Josh asked.

"The airport told me the plane landed, Josh."

"And Maureen Higgins said she picked him up," Ruth Rose added.

"Okay, so your glass is the airport," Josh said. "Keep going, Dink."

Dink slid his sandwich plate over next to his glass. "My plate is Maureen's taxi." He put a cookie on the plate. "The cookie is Wallis Wallace getting into the taxi."

Dink slid the plate over to the opened potato chip bag. "This bag is the hotel." He walked the Wallis Wallace cookie from the plate into the bag.

Dink looked at Josh and Ruth Rose. "But what happened to Wallis Wallace after he walked into the lobby?"

**After Reading Pages 56 and 57**

**❶ Understand:** Summarizing

What did the kids know about Wallis Wallace?
(Wallis Wallace arrived at the airport. He took a taxi to the hotel. He checked into the hotel . . . )

"I'll tell you what happened," Josh said. He lined up four cookies in a row. "This little cookie is Mr. Paskey. These three are Maureen, Mr. Linkletter, and Olivia Nugent."

60

Josh looked up and waggled his eyebrows. "I think these four cookies planned the kidnapping *together!*"

Ruth Rose laughed. "Josh, Mr. Paskey and Livvy Nugent are friends of ours. Do you really think they planned this big kidnapping? And can you see Mr. Linkletter and my baby-sitter pulling off a kidnapping together?"

Josh ate a potato chip. "Well, maybe not. But *someone* kidnapped the guy!"

"Our trail led us to the hotel, and then it ended," Dink said. "What I want to know is, if Wallis Wallace isn't in his room, where is he?"

Dink nibbled on a cookie thoughtfully. "I'm getting a headache trying to sort it all out."

Ruth Rose dug in Dink's backpack and brought out three Wallis Wallace books. "I have an idea." She handed books to Dink and Josh and kept one.

## After Reading Page 60

❶ **Remember:** Identifying—Where
Where did the trail of clues end?
(The clues ended at the hotel.)

❷ **Apply:** Inferring, Explaining
What do you think Ruth Rose's idea is?
(Maybe they will find some clues in Wallis Wallace's books . . . )

### CHAPTER 7 INSTRUCTIONS

Students read Chapter 7, pages 61–65, without the teacher, independently or with partners.

### COMPREHENSION PROCESSES

**Understand, Analyze**

### PROCEDURES FOR READING ON YOUR OWN

1. **Getting Ready**

   Have students turn to page 61.

2. **Setting a Purpose**

   **Summarizing, Drawing Conclusions**

   Before students begin reading, say something like:

   As you read the next pages, try to answer these questions:
   - What was Ruth Rose's idea?
   - What new clues did the kids find?
   - Why might Room 302 be a clue?

3. **Reading on Your Own: Partner or Whisper Reading**
   - Have students take turns reading every other page with a partner or have students whisper read pages 61–65 on their own.
   - Continue having students track each word with their fingers.

4. **Comprehension and Skill Work**

   Tell students they will do Case Log Entry 6 and Comprehension and Skill Activities 6a and 6b after they read on their own. Guide practice, as needed. For teacher directions, see pages 102–105.

5. **Homework 6: New Passage**

> **PREP NOTE**
>
> **Setting a Purpose**
>
> Write questions on a chalkboard, white board, or large piece of paper before working with your small group.

"What're these for?" Dink asked.

"Josh made me think of something Wallis Wallace wrote in *The Mystery in the Museum*," Ruth Rose said. "He said the more you know about the victim, the easier it is to figure out who did the crime."

She turned to the back cover of her book. "So let's try to find out more about our victim. Listen to this." She started reading out loud. "'When not writing, the author likes to work in the garden. Naturally, Wallis Wallace's favorite color is green.'"

"Fine," said Josh, "but how does knowing his favorite color help us find him, Ruth Rose?"

"I don't know, but maybe if we read more about him, we'll discover some clues," Ruth Rose said. "What does it say on the back of your book?"

Josh flipped the book over and began

*62*

reading. "'Wallis Wallace lives in a castle called Moose Manor.'" He looked up. "We already knew he lived in a castle. I don't see any clues yet, you guys."

Ruth Rose stared at Josh. "You know, something is bugging me, but I can't figure out what it is. Something someone said today, maybe." She shook her head. "Anyway, read yours, Dink."

Dink read from the back cover of his book. "'Wallis Wallace gives money from writing books to help preserve the wild animals that live in Maine.'"

"Okay, he gives money away to save animals, lives in a castle, and grows a bunch of green stuff," Josh said, counting on his fingers. "Still no clues."

Josh took another cookie. "But I just thought of something." He began slowly munching on the cookie.

Dink raised his eyebrows. "Are you going to tell us, Josh?"

"Well, I was thinking about Room 302. Remember, someone signed the register right after Wallis Wallace checked into Room 303? And the signature was all smudged? And then Olivia Nugent—"

"—told us that Room 302 had a Do Not Disturb sign on it!" Ruth Rose interrupted. "Livvy never went into that room at all!"

Just then Dink's mother drove up the driveway. She got out of the car, waved, and started walking toward the picnic table.

"Oh, no!" Dink said. "If Mom finds out I'm trying to find a kidnapper, she won't let me out of the house! Don't say anything, okay?"

"Can't I even say hi?" Josh asked.

Dink threw a potato chip at Josh. "Say hi, then shut up about you-know-what!"

64

"Hi, Mrs. Duncan!" Josh said, sliding a look at Dink.

"Hi, kids. How was the book signing? Tell me all about Wallis Wallace, Dink. Is he as wonderful as you expected?"

Dink stared at his mother. He didn't want to lie. But if he told her the truth, she wouldn't let him keep looking for Wallis Wallace. And Dink had a sudden feeling that they were very close to finding him.

*We can't stop now!* he thought. He looked at his mother and grinned stupidly.

"Dink? Honey? Why is your mouth open?"

He closed his mouth. *Think, Dink!* he ordered himself.

Suddenly Josh knocked over his lemonade glass. The sticky cold liquid spilled into Dink's lap.

Dink let out a yowl and jumped up.

"Gee, sorry!" said Josh.

"Paper towels to the rescue!" Dink's mother ran toward the house.

"Good thinking, Josh," Dink said, wiping at his wet jeans. "But did you have to spill it on *me?* You had the whole yard!"

Josh grinned. "Some people are never satisfied. I got you out of hot water, didn't I?"

"Right into cold lemonade," Ruth Rose said.

Dink blotted his jeans with a handful of paper napkins. "Come on. Let's go meet Mavis before my mom comes back. There's something weird happening on the third floor of the Shangri-la!"

## ENTRY 6

### COMPREHENSION PROCESSES

**Understand, Analyze**

### WRITING TRAITS

**Conventions—Capital, Period**

### PROCEDURES

Discuss each step. Then have students complete the page independently.

**Note Taking: Summarizing—Basic Instructions**
- Have students read the case notes and fill in the blanks. Remind students to use capitals for proper names.
- Have students read the "I THINK . . . " box and fill in the bubble with the correct answer.

**Identifying—What, Who, When**
**Drawing Conclusions**
**Sentence Completion**

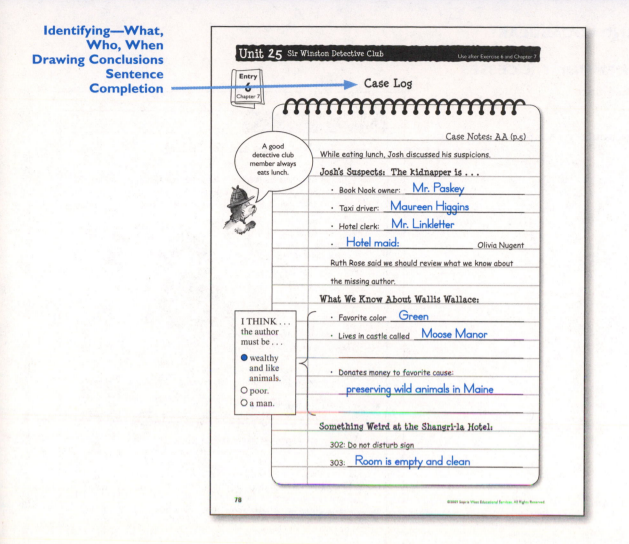

Entry 6
Chapter 7

**Unit 25** Sir Winston Detective Club     Use after Exercise 6 and Chapter 7

## Case Log

Case Notes: AA (p.5)

*A good detective club member always eats lunch.*

While eating lunch, Josh discussed his suspicions.

**Josh's Suspects: The kidnapper is . . .**

- Book Nook owner:   Mr. Paskey
- Taxi driver:   Maureen Higgins
- Hotel clerk:   Mr. Linkletter
- Hotel maid:       Olivia Nugent

Ruth Rose said we should review what we know about

the missing author.

**What We Know About Wallis Wallace:**

- Favorite color   Green
- Lives in castle called   Moose Manor

I THINK . . .
the author
must be . . .

- ● wealthy and like animals.
- ○ poor.
- ○ a man.

- Donates money to favorite cause:

   preserving wild animals in Maine

**Something Weird at the Shangri-la Hotel:**

302: Do not disturb sign

303:   Room is empty and clean

78            ©2007 Sopris West Educational Services. All Rights Reserved.

### GENRE AND VOCABULARY

### COMPREHENSION PROCESSES

Apply, Evaluate

Using Vocabulary—suspicious, opinion
Responding

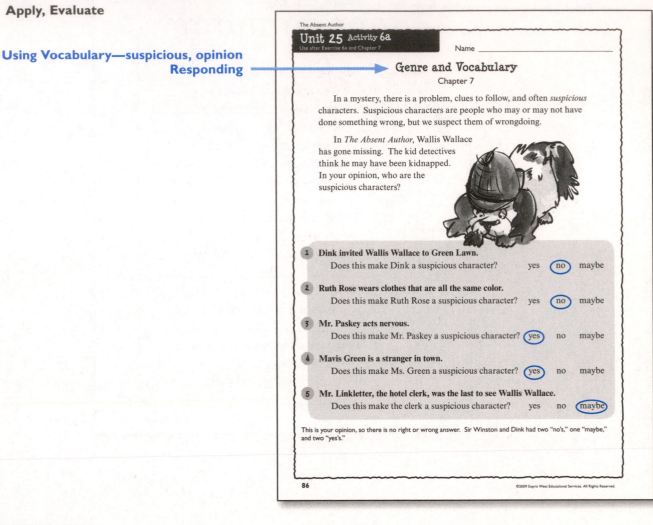

The Absent Author

**Unit 25** Activity 6a
Use after Exercise 6a and Chapter 7

Name _____

### Genre and Vocabulary
#### Chapter 7

In a mystery, there is a problem, clues to follow, and often *suspicious* characters. Suspicious characters are people who may or may not have done something wrong, but we suspect them of wrongdoing.

In *The Absent Author*, Wallis Wallace has gone missing. The kid detectives think he may have been kidnapped. In your opinion, who are the suspicious characters?

1  **Dink invited Wallis Wallace to Green Lawn.**
   Does this make Dink a suspicious character?     yes    (no)    maybe

2  **Ruth Rose wears clothes that are all the same color.**
   Does this make Ruth Rose a suspicious character?     yes    (no)    maybe

3  **Mr. Paskey acts nervous.**
   Does this make Mr. Paskey a suspicious character?    (yes)    no    maybe

4  **Mavis Green is a stranger in town.**
   Does this make Ms. Green a suspicious character?    (yes)    no    maybe

5  **Mr. Linkletter, the hotel clerk, was the last to see Wallis Wallace.**
   Does this make the clerk a suspicious character?     yes    no    (maybe)

This is your opinion, so there is no right or wrong answer. Sir Winston and Dink had two "no's," one "maybe," and two "yes's."

86

©2009 Sopris West Educational Services. All Rights Reserved.

### PROCEDURES

For each step, demonstrate and guide practice, as needed. Then have students complete the page independently.

**Characterization: Selection Response—Specific Instructions** (Items 1–5)
Have students read the introduction and each sentence. Have students circle yes, no, or maybe for each character.

## *READ WELL* LITERARY AWARDS

### COMPREHENSION PROCESSES

**Understand, Evaluate**

**Viewing, Responding, Explaining** →

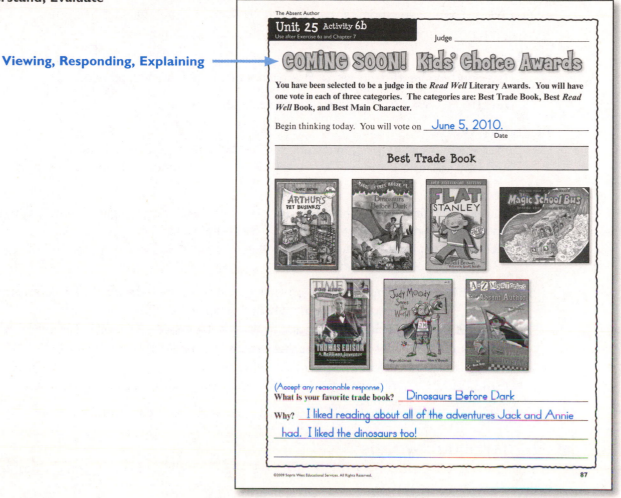

The Absent Author

**Unit 25** Activity **6b**
Use after Exercise 6a and Chapter 7

Judge _____

## COMING SOON! Kids' Choice Awards

You have been selected to be a judge in the *Read Well* Literary Awards. You will have one vote in each of three categories. The categories are: Best Trade Book, Best *Read Well* Book, and Best Main Character.

Begin thinking today. You will vote on __June 5, 2010.__
                                                          Date

### Best Trade Book

(Accept any reasonable response.)
**What is your favorite trade book?** __Dinosaurs Before Dark__

**Why?** __I liked reading about all of the adventures Jack and Annie__ __had. I liked the dinosaurs too!__

©2009 Sopris West Educational Services. All Rights Reserved.                    87

### Personal Response: Creative Writing—Specific Instructions

Have students choose their favorite trade book in the program, then write one or two sentences telling why it is their favorite.

**CHECKOUT OPPORTUNITY**

Listen to your students read individually while others work.

**1 SOUND REVIEW**

**2 ACCURACY AND FLUENCY BUILDING**
- For each task, have students say any underlined part, then read the word.
- Set a pace. Then have students read the whole words in each task and column.
- Provide repeated practice, building accuracy first, then fluency.

**D1. Affixes**

Have students read each word. Use each word in a sentence, as needed.

**timidly**      Sue wasn't courageous or confident. She behaved . . . *timidly*.

**E1. Tricky Words**
- For each Tricky Word, have students use the sounds and word parts they know to silently sound out the word. Use the word in a sentence to help with pronunciation.

**cough**
Look at the first word. This word is tricky, but I think you can figure it out. Silently sound it out, then thumbs up when you know it. Read the word.  (cough)
It's important to stay home when you have a bad cold and a . . . *cough*.
Read the word three times.  (cough, cough, cough)

| | |
|---|---|
| **coughing** | When Ana got sick, her throat was sore because she kept . . . *coughing*. |
| **untie** | The knots were really tight. Jean couldn't . . . *untie* . . . them. |
| **untied** | Jean kept trying and finally got the knots . . . *untied*. |
| **drawer** | Mom said to put these socks in your . . . *drawer*. |
| **tongue** | When a dog pants, it sticks out its . . . *tongue*. |
| **unusual** | When something is different from what is normal or usual, it is . . . *unusual*. |

- Have students go back and read the whole words in the column.

**3 MULTISYLLABIC WORDS**

For each word, have students read the syllables, then the whole word. Use the word in a sentence, as appropriate.

| | |
|---|---|
| **muffled** | Roxanne couldn't hear Paula. Paula's voice was . . . *muffled* . . . by her scarf. |
| **mercy** | Another way to say "Oh, dear!" is . . . *Mercy!* |
| **itinerary** | I couldn't remember where my next meeting was, so I looked at my . . . *itinerary*. |
| **recognize** | Amy wore a disguise, so I didn't . . . *recognize* . . . her. |
| **register** | When you check into a hotel, you sign the hotel . . . *register*. |
| **definitely** | Brandon asked if Molly wanted to go to the dance. She said . . . "*Definitely*." |

**4 NAMES AND PLACES**

**5 MORPHOGRAPHS AND AFFIXES**
- Have students read the underlined part, then the whole word.
- Repeat practice with whole words, mixing group and individual turns.
  Build accuracy, then fluency.

**⑥ GENERALIZATION: READING NEW WORDS IN PARAGRAPHS**

- Have students read the paragraph silently, then out loud. Tell students to use the sounds and word parts they know to read any difficult words.
- Repeat practice, as needed.

---

The Absent Author

## Unit 25 Exercise 7
Use before Chapters 8 and 9

**1. SOUND REVIEW** Use selected Sound Cards from Units 1–19.

**2. ACCURACY/FLUENCY BUILDING** For each column, have students say any underlined part, then read each word. Next, have them read the column.

| A1 Mixed Practice | B1 Word Endings | C1 Compound Words | D1 Affixes | E1 Tricky Words |
|---|---|---|---|---|
| curly | smudged | forehead | nearly | cough |
| keys | pointed | eyeglasses | smoothly | coughing |
| bunch | trooped | headache | sweetly | untie |
| jaw | glasses | doorknob | timidly | untied |
| disturb | | | spotlessly | |
| arrow | jiggle | | vividly | drawer |
| | jiggling | | | tongue |
| | | | | unusual |

**3. MULTISYLLABIC WORDS** Have students read each word part, then read each whole word.

| | | | | |
|---|---|---|---|---|
| Ⓐ | muf·fled | muffled | mer·cy | mercy |
| Ⓑ | i·tin·e·rar·y | itinerary | re·cog·nize | recognize |
| Ⓒ | re·gi·ster | register | def·i·nite·ly | definitely |

**4. NAMES AND PLACES** Have students use the sounds and word parts they know to figure out the words.

| Officer Fallon | Maine | Miss Nugent | Adam's |
|---|---|---|---|

**5. MORPHOGRAPHS AND AFFIXES** Have students read the underlined word part, then the word.

| goodness | disappeared | replaced | expression | elevator |
|---|---|---|---|---|

**6. GENERALIZATION** Have students read the paragraph silently, then out loud. (New words: cottage, draped)

Ruth was so excited. She had just purchased her first home—a cute little cottage in the woods. She was eager to decorate. She had already bought some curtains, which she draped over the living room windows. But she still needed curtains for the other rooms and some furniture.

---

**APPROPRIATE CORRECTIONS**
**(Reminder)**

Write any difficult words on a board or clipboard.

**Single-Syllable Pattern Words**
Have students identify the difficult sound, then sound out and say the word.

**Multisyllabic Words**
Draw loops under each word part and then guide practice with your hand.

**Tricky Words**
Have students sound out or read the word by parts, then say the word. Next have students say, spell, and say the word.

After gently correcting a word with the group, go on to other tasks or words. Return to the difficult word at least three times.

## COMPREHENSION PROCESSES

**Understand, Apply**

## PROCEDURES

**Introducing Vocabulary**

★**muffled** ★**vividly** ★**tied up, definitely** ★**assume**

- For each vocabulary word, have students read the word by parts, then read the whole word.
- Read the student-friendly explanations to students as they follow with their fingers. Then have students use the vocabulary word by following the gray text.
- Review and discuss the illustrations.

*Note*: Student vocabulary pages for this unit are found in the students' *Exercise Book 4*.

**USING VOCABULARY**

The Absent Author

# Unit 25 Vocabulary 7
Use after Exercise 7

| ★**muf·fled** | Francis could hear *muffled* voices in the next room. |
|---|---|
| A sound is **muffled** when it cannot be heard clearly. It is softer or quieter. | What did those voices sound like?**1** |
| ★**viv·id·ly** | Albert *vividly* remembers the first day he walked into his new class. He remembers who was there, what the teacher said, and what the other kids said. |
| **Vividly** means clearly. | What do you vividly remember?**2** |
| ★**tied up** | My mom called to say she was still *tied up* at work. |
| **Tied up** is an expression that means very busy. Someone who is tied up cannot do anything else. | Why will my mom be coming home late?**3** |

**1** **Understand:** Defining and Using Vocabulary—muffled  (The muffled voices could not be heard clearly. They were soft and quiet.)

**2** **Apply:** Making Connections; Using Vocabulary—vividly  (I vividly remember my sixth birthday . . . )

**3** **Apply:** Using Vocabulary—tied up  (Your mom will be coming home late because she is very busy and can't leave.)

★ = New in this unit

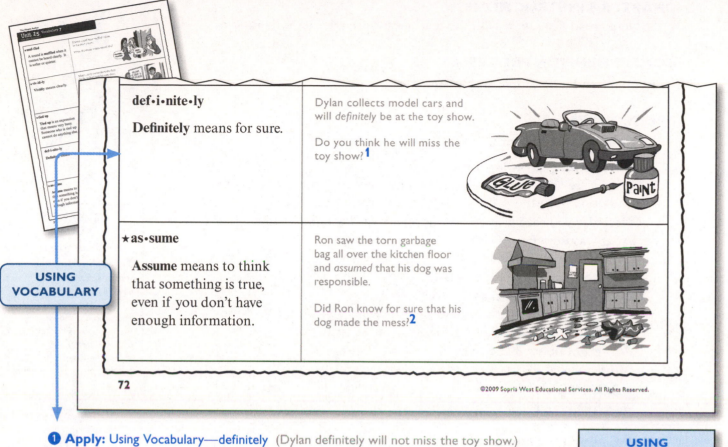

def·i·nite·ly

**Definitely** means for sure.

Dylan collects model cars and will *definitely* be at the toy show.

Do you think he will miss the toy show?[1]

★as·sume

**Assume** means to think that something is true, even if you don't have enough information.

Ron saw the torn garbage bag all over the kitchen floor and *assumed* that his dog was responsible.

Did Ron know for sure that his dog made the mess?[2]

72

**USING VOCABULARY**

❶ **Apply:** Using Vocabulary—definitely  (Dylan definitely will not miss the toy show.)

❷ **Understand:** Using Vocabulary—assume, responsible  (Ron didn't know for sure that his dog was responsible.)

**USING VOCABULARY**

Be enthusiastic about learning new words. Keep a running list of words you would like to use and encourage students to use. Keep the list handy when you are teaching. Put students' names on the board to acknowledge use of a word. Say things like:

Wow! [Peg] used the word *assume* when she asked about tonight's homework assignment. That's definitely a great way to use a vocabulary word!

## CHAPTER 8 INSTRUCTIONS

Students read Chapter 8 with the teacher and Chapter 9 on their own.

## COMPREHENSION PROCESSES

**Remember, Understand, Apply, Analyze**

## PROCEDURES

**1. Reviewing Chapter 7**

**Summarizing, Drawing Conclusions**

Quickly review what has happened in the story so far. Discuss the questions from the previous Setting a Purpose. Say something like:

Yesterday you read pages 61–65 on your own. Let's see what you found out. What was Ruth Rose's idea?

(They should try to find out more about Wallis Wallace. The more they know about the victim, the easier it is to figure out who did the crime.)

What did the kids learn about Wallis Wallace?

(Wallis lives in a castle called Moose Manor in Maine, he likes to garden, he likes the wild animals of Maine. His favorite color is green . . . )

Why might Room 302 be a clue?

(Whoever was in that room checked in right after Wallis Wallace. The person signed in with a smudged name so no one could read it. The room had a "Do Not Disturb" sign on the door . . . )

> **REPEATED READINGS**
>
> **Prosody**
>
> On the second reading, students practice developing prosody— phrasing and expression. Research has shown that prosody is related to both fluency and comprehension.

**2. Introducing Chapter 8**

**Predicting**
Say something like:

I can't wait to find out what happens when they go back to the hotel.

What do you think will happen when they get there?

(They will look for Wallis Wallace. They will look in his room . . . )

**3. First Reading**
- Ask questions and discuss the text as indicated by the blue text in this guide.
- Mix group and individual turns, independent of your voice. Have students work toward a group accuracy goal of 0–6 errors. Quietly keep track of errors made by all students in the group.
- After reading the story, practice any difficult words. Repeat, if students have not reached the accuracy goal.

**4. Second Reading, Short Passage Practice: Developing Prosody**
- Demonstrate expressive, fluent reading of the first paragraph. Read at a rate slightly faster than the students' rate.
- Guide practice with your voice.
- Provide individual turns while others track with their fingers and whisper read.
- Repeat with one paragraph at a time.

Dink's jeans were nearly dry by the time they reached the hotel. Mavis was waiting out front.

"How was your lunch?" she asked timidly.

"Fine, thanks," Dink said. "We talked it over, and we think there's something fishy going on on the third floor of this hotel."

Suddenly Mavis began coughing. She held up her scarf in front of her mouth.

Dink noticed that the letters on the

66

scarf were tiny M's. "Are you okay?" he asked.

"Should I run in and get you some water?" asked Josh.

Mavis took off her glasses and shook her head. "No, I'm fine, thank you. Dear me, I don't know what happened! Now, what were you saying about the third floor?"

"We think Wallis Wallace may be up there," Ruth Rose said. She reminded Mavis about the smudged signature for Room 302 and the Do Not Disturb sign on the door.

Mavis replaced her eyeglasses. "Mercy! What do you think we should do?"

"Follow me!" Dink said. For the second time, they all trooped into the hotel lobby.

Mr. Linkletter watched them from behind the counter.

## After Reading Page 66

❶ **Apply:** Inferring, Explaining, Defining and Using Idioms and Expressions—smelled fishy
The kids think something is fishy or smells fishy on the third floor of the hotel. What does that mean?
(They think Wallace is on the third floor of the hotel. They think something isn't right on the third floor of the hotel.)

68

"Hi," Dink said. "Remember us?"

"Vividly," Mr. Linkletter said.

"Wallis Wallace checked into Room 303, right?"

"That is correct," said Mr. Linkletter.

"Well, we talked to the maid who cleaned that room," Dink went on. "She told us no one slept in it."

"You spoke to Olivia Nugent? When? How?"

"We have our ways," Josh said.

"So," Dink went on, "we think Wallis Wallace disappeared right here in this hotel."

"And Wallis Wallace is a *very* famous writer," Ruth Rose reminded Mr. Linkletter. "Millions of kids are waiting to read his next book," she added sweetly.

Mr. Linkletter's sad eyes grew large. He swallowed and his Adam's apple bobbed up and down. He rubbed his

forehead as though he had a headache.

Then Dink told Mr. Linkletter about Room 302. "Miss Nugent said there was a Do Not Disturb sign on the door."

Ruth Rose pointed to the register. "See? The signature is all smudged!"

"We think the kidnappers are hiding Wallis Wallace in that room!" Josh said.

At the word "kidnappers," Mr. Linkletter closed his eyes. He opened a drawer, took out a bottle of headache pills, and put one on his tongue.

"Just to be on the safe side, perhaps we should check both rooms, Mr. Linkletter," Mavis said quietly.

"It'll just take a minute," Dink said.

Mr. Linkletter let out a big sigh. "Very well, but this is most unusual. Things run very smoothly at the Shangrila."

They all got into the elevator. No one spoke. Dink watched Mr. Linkletter jig-

## After Reading Page 68

❶ **Understand:** Using Vocabulary—vividly; **Analyze:** Drawing Conclusions
Dink asked Mr. Linkletter if he remembered them. Mr. Linkletter said, "Vividly." Why do you think Mr. Linkletter remembered the kids vividly?
(The kids had asked a lot of questions. They had wanted to bend the rules.  They wanted Mr. Linkletter to disturb Wallis Wallace . . . )

## After Reading Page 69

❶ **Understand:** Explaining
How did the kids get Mr. Linkletter to take them to the third floor?
(They told him they thought Wallis Wallace was kidnapped and that the kidnappers were hiding him in Room 302.)

❷ **Apply:** Inferring, Explaining; Using Vocabulary—distressed
Why did Mr. Linkletter take a headache pill?
(He was distressed.  If Wallis Wallace was kidnapped at his hotel, no one will want to stay there.  It will be in the newspapers . . . )

70

gling his bunch of keys. Mr. Linkletter kept his eyes on the little arrow telling them which floor they were on.

The elevator door opened on the third floor. Mr. Linkletter unlocked Room 303. "Most unusual," he muttered.

The room was empty and spotlessly clean. "Strange, very strange," Mr. Linkletter said.

They moved to Room 302, where a Do Not Disturb sign still hung on the doorknob.

Mr. Linkletter knocked. They all leaned toward the door.

"Listen, I hear a voice!" Josh said.

"What's it saying?" Ruth Rose asked.

Then they all heard it.

The voice was muffled, but it was definitely yelling, "HELP!"

## After Reading Page 70

❶ **Apply:** Inferring, Explaining
Why did Mr. Linkletter say "Most unusual" after opening the door to Room 303?
(The room was empty. It was clean. It looked like no one had been there.)

## After Reading Page 71

❶ **Remember:** Identifying—What
What did the voice in Room 302 say?
(Help!)

## CHAPTER 9 INSTRUCTIONS

Students read Chapter 9 without the teacher, independently or with partners.

## COMPREHENSION PROCESSES

**Understand, Apply**

## PROCEDURES FOR READING ON YOUR OWN

### 1. Getting Ready

Have students turn to page 72.

### 2. Setting a Purpose

**Using Vocabulary—suspense; Predicting; Explaining**

Before students begin reading, say something like:

The author left us in suspense at the end of the last chapter. What do you think we're going to find out in this chapter?

(We'll find out who was yelling for help, whether the kids were right . . . )

I can't wait to find out what happens. As you read, think about these questions:

- What did they find in Room 302?
- What happened to Wallis Wallace?
- At the end, what did Ruth Rose say?

> **PREP NOTE**
>
> **Setting a Purpose**
>
> Write questions on a chalkboard, white board, or large piece of paper before working with your small group.

### 3. Reading on Your Own: Partner or Whisper Reading

- Have students take turns reading every other page with a partner or have students whisper read Chapter 9 on their own.
- Continue having students track each word with their fingers.

### 4. Comprehension and Skill Work

Tell students they will do Case Log Entry 7 and Comprehension and Skill Activity 7 after they read on their own. Guide practice, as needed. For teacher directions, see pages 117–119.

### 5. Homework 7: New Passage

## Chapter 9

Mr. Linkletter unlocked the door and shoved it open.

A man with curly blond hair stared back at them. He was sitting in a chair with his feet tied in front of him. His arms were tied behind his back. A towel was wrapped around his mouth.

"Oh, my goodness!" Mr. Linkletter cried.

Everyone rushed into the room.

Dink ran behind the chair to untie the man's hands while Josh untied his

72

74

feet.

Mavis unwrapped the towel from around his face.

"Thank goodness you got here!" the man said. "I'm Wallis Wallace. Someone knocked on my door last night. A voice said he was from room service. When I opened the door, two men dragged me in here and tied me up."

He looked at Dink. "You're Dink Duncan! I recognize you from the picture you sent. How did you find me?"

"We followed your itinerary," Dink said. He showed Mr. Wallace the sheet of paper. "We got it from Mr. Paskey and used it as a trail. The trail led us to this room!"

"I'm so sorry I missed the book signing," Wallis Wallace said. "As you can see, I was a bit tied up."

He smiled. Then he rubbed his jaw. "My mouth is sore from that towel. I

can't believe I was kidnapped! And I can't wait to get back to my safe little cottage in Maine."

"Can you describe the two guys who kidnapped you?" Dink asked. "We should tell Officer Fallon so he can try to find them."

Wallis Wallace stared at Dink. "The two guys? Oh...well, um, I don't think I'll—"

"HEY!" Ruth Rose suddenly yelled.

Everyone looked at her.

"What's the matter?" asked Dink. "You look funny, Ruth Rose."

Ruth Rose was staring at the red scarf draped around Mavis's neck. She pointed at the man who'd been tied up. "You're not Wallis Wallace!"

Then she looked at Mavis Green. "*You* are," she said quietly.

## ENTRY 7

### COMPREHENSION PROCESSES

**Understand, Analyze**

### WRITING TRAITS

**Conventions—Capital, Period**
**Presentation**

**Identifying—What; Explaining Drawing Conclusions; Sentence Completion; Sentence Writing Using Vocabulary—suspicion**

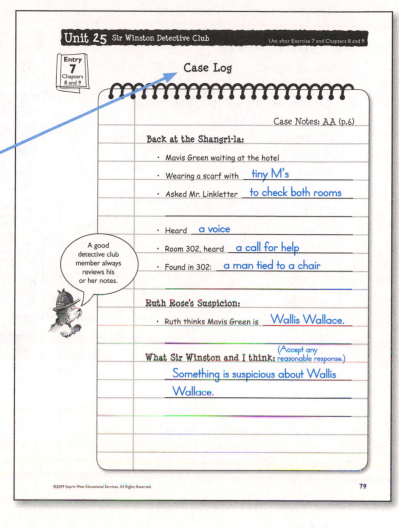

### PROCEDURES

Discuss each step. Then have students complete the page independently.

**Note Taking: Summarizing—Basic Instructions**

Have students read the case notes and fill in the blanks. Remind students to use capitals for beginning a sentence and for proper names and a period at the end of a sentence.

### BEST *READ WELL* STORYBOOK

### COMPREHENSION PROCESSES

Understand, Evaluate, Create

### WRITING TRAITS

Ideas and Content
Word Choice
Organization—Topic Sentence,
Supporting Details
Conventions—Complete Sentence,
Capital, Period
Presentation

Viewing

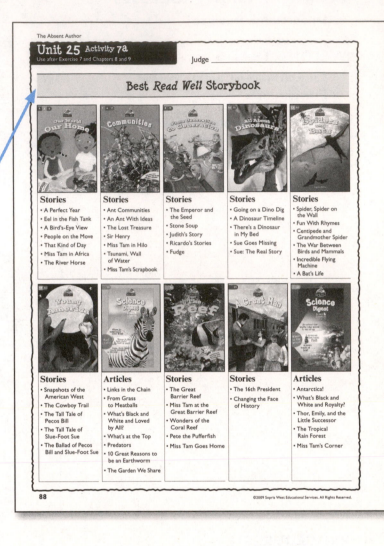

### PROCEDURES

For each step, demonstrate and guide practice, as needed. Then have students complete the
page independently.

**Personal Response: Hierarchy Chart, Paragraph Writing—Specific Instructions**

• Using Activity 7a, have students choose their favorite *Read Well* storybook in the program.

• Have students complete the main idea sentence on Activity 7b with their choice.

• Have students write three supporting details in the chart (7b) to explain why it is
their favorite.

• Have students write a main-idea/supporting-detail paragraph (7b) using the information in
the graphic organizer.

## BEST *READ WELL* STORYBOOK

**Using Graphic Organizer; Responding**
**Explaining—Supporting Details**
**Generating Ideas; Sentence Writing**

The Absent Author

**Unit 25** Activity **7b**
Use after Exercise 7 and Chapters 8 and 9

Name _____

### Best *Read Well* Storybook

Critic's Corner: In My Opinion

by _Matt_____

★ ★ ★ ★ ★

**Topic/Main Idea:** The best of the *Read Well* storybooks was
_The Reef._____
_____

**Supporting Details:** Why    (Accept any reasonable response.)

| The Great Barrier Reef is alive. | The reef has interesting food chains. | Miss Tam had fun scuba diving. |

(Accept any reasonable response.)

**In my opinion,** _the best Read Well storybook was The Reef. I_
_learned about the Great Barrier Reef. Did you know that it is_
_alive? I also read about the food chains in the reef. Miss Tam_
_made me laugh when she went scuba diving. It was a great_
_storybook!_
_____
_____

89

### ❶ SOUND REVIEW

Have students read the sounds and key word phrases. Work for accuracy, then fluency.

**MULTISYLLABIC WORDS CORRECTION PROCEDURE**

If students make an error, put the word on the board. Draw loops under each syllable and guide practice with your hand. Have students say each syllable then read the whole word.

### ❷ ACCURACY AND FLUENCY BUILDING

- For each task, have students say any underlined part, then read the word.
- Set a pace. Then have students read the whole words in each task and column.
- Provide repeated practice, building accuracy first, then fluency.

#### B1. Multisyllabic Words

Have students read each whole word. Use each word in a sentence, as needed.

#### E1. Tricky Words

- For each Tricky Word, have students use the sounds and word parts they know to silently sound out the word. Use the word in a sentence to help with pronunciation.

| | |
|---|---|
| **cough** | Rihana's mom went to the doctor. She wanted medicine for her . . . *cough*. |
| **brilliant** | My big brother passed all his exams because he's . . . *brilliant*. |
| **untied** | Jade tripped over her shoelaces when they became . . . *untied*. |
| **double** | The twins looked just like each other. They were each other's . . . *double*. |
| **honest** | Please don't tell lies. Be . . . *honest*. |

- Have students go back and read the whole words in the column.

### ❸ MULTISYLLABIC WORDS

For each word, have students read the syllables, then the whole word. Use the word in a sentence, as appropriate.

| | |
|---|---|
| **dedicate** | The writer decided to . . . *dedicate* . . . his book to his friend. |
| **reserve** | When you save something for later, you . . . *reserve* . . . it. |
| **forgive** | Cass was mean to her friend. Cass was sorry and asked her friend to . . . *forgive* . . . her. |
| **completely** | We didn't have any idea where we were. We were . . . *completely* . . . lost. |
| **assume** | I can't see my brother's bike. He's gone to school, I . . . *assume*. |
| **investigate** | A detective's job is to find out the truth, or to . . . *investigate*. |

### ❹ WORDS IN CONTEXT

For each word, have students use the sounds and word parts they know to silently sound out the word. Then have students read the sentence. Assist, as needed.

### ❺ NAMES AND PLACES

- Tell students these are people and places they will be reading about in the story.
- Have students use the sounds and word parts they know to figure out the words. Use the words in sentences, as needed.

### ❻ GENERALIZATION: READING NEW WORDS IN PARAGRAPHS

- Have students read the paragraph silently, then out loud. Tell students to use the sounds and word parts they know to read any difficult words.
- Repeat practice, as needed.

The Absent Author

## Unit 25 Exercise 8
Use before Chapter 10

**1. SOUND REVIEW** Have students review sounds for accuracy, then for fluency.

| | | | | | |
|---|---|---|---|---|---|
| **A** | -y as in fly | a as in ago | OO as in book | OW as in cow | ea as in eagle |
| **B** | ir | o_e | ay | i_e | ou |

**2. ACCURACY/FLUENCY BUILDING** For each column, have students say any underlined part, then read each word. Next, have them read the column.

| A1<br>Mixed Practice | B1<br>Multisyllabic Words | C1<br>Word Endings | D1<br>Word Endings | E1<br>Tricky Words |
|---|---|---|---|---|
| exc<u>u</u>se | cottage | handle | <u>lobster</u>s | cough |
| <u>au</u>thor | disguise | handling | telephon<u>ed</u> | brilliant |
| blon<u>d</u> | triple | | smudg<u>ed</u> | untied |
| a<u>l</u>ong | timid | invite | <u>kidnapping</u> | double |
| nutt<u>y</u> | explanation | inviting | <u>prepar</u>ed | honest |

**3. MULTISYLLABIC WORDS** Have students read each word part, then read each whole word.

| | | | | |
|---|---|---|---|---|
| **A** | ded•i•cate | dedicate | re•serve | reserve |
| **B** | for•give | forgive | com•plete•ly | completely |
| **C** | as•sume | assume | in•ves•ti•gate | investigate |

**4. WORDS IN CONTEXT** Have students use the sounds they know and then the sentences to pronounce each underlined word.

| | | |
|---|---|---|
| **A** | scheme (skeem) | He came up with a <u>scheme</u> to make money. |
| **B** | sus•pi•cious | Wallace was <u>suspicious</u> of the nervous man with a fake beard. |

**5. NAMES AND PLACES** Have students use the sounds and word parts they know to figure out the words.

| | | |
|---|---|---|
| Connecticut | Moose Manor | Maine |

**6. GENERALIZATION** Have students read the paragraph silently, then out loud. (New words: barrettes, mass, public, fuddy-duddy)

Mavis put on her favorite dress and put pretty silver barrettes into her mass of wild curls. She was really looking forward to going out in public now that she had her braces off. The first thing she wanted to do was go to the TV station and dance on her favorite show, "You Can Dance!" Her Aunt Josephine, who Mavis thought was a fuddy-duddy, told Mavis, "Young ladies should not dance to rock music on television!"

73

## COMPREHENSION PROCESSES

**Understand, Apply, Analyze**

## PROCEDURES

**Introducing Vocabulary**

disguise ★ dedicate ★ cat's out of the bag, brilliant

- For each vocabulary word, have students read the word by parts, then read the whole word.
- Read the student-friendly explanations to students as they follow with their fingers. Then have students use the vocabulary word by following the gray text.
- Review and discuss the illustrations.
  *Note*: Student vocabulary pages for this unit are found in the students' *Exercise Book 4*.

**USING VOCABULARY**

The Absent Author

# Unit 25 Vocabulary 8
Use after Exercise 8

| **dis•guise**<br><br>Something that hides the way you look is called a **disguise**. | The woman wore a wig and glasses. She had on a …**1**<br><br>Why do you think she wore a *disguise?***2** | |
| **★ded•i•cate**<br><br>When you **dedicate** a book to someone, you say that it has been written for someone special. | The author *dedicated* his book to his parents. He wanted to thank them for their help.<br><br>If you wrote a book, who would you dedicate it to? **3** | *To Mom and Dad who helped me so much in writing this book* |

**1 Understand:** Using Vocabulary—disguise  (disguise)

**2 Apply:** Using Vocabulary—disguise, recognize  (She wore a disguise because she didn't want anyone to recognize her.)

**3 Apply:** Using Vocabulary—dedicate  (I would dedicate it to my reading teacher . . . )

★ = New in this unit

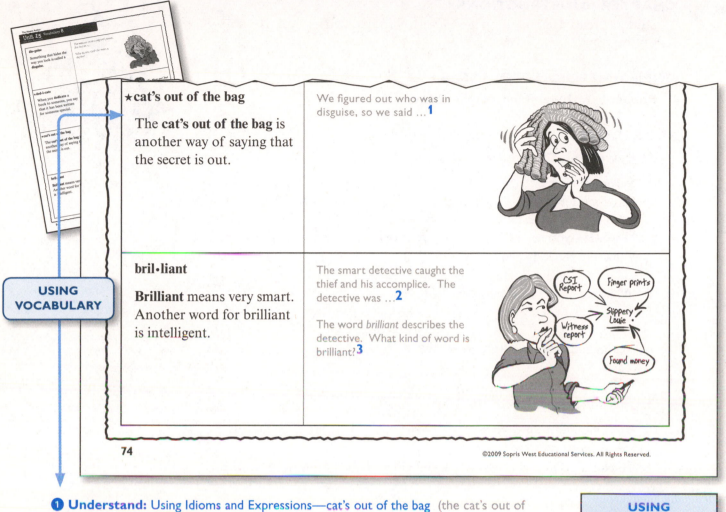

**USING VOCABULARY**

❶ **Understand:** Using Idioms and Expressions—cat's out of the bag  (the cat's out of the bag)

❷ **Apply:** Using Vocabulary—brilliant  (brilliant)

❸ **Analyze:** Classifying; **Apply:** Using Vocabulary—brilliant  (Brilliant is an adjective.)

**USING VOCABULARY**

Be enthusiastic about learning new words. Keep a running list of words you would like to use and encourage students to use. Keep the list handy when you are teaching. Put students' names on the board to acknowledge use of a word. Say things like:

Wow! [Keith] used the expression *cat's out of the bag* when everyone figured out it was his birthday. That's a great way to use an expression!

### CHAPTER 10 INSTRUCTIONS

Students read Chapter 10, pages 76–81 with the teacher and pages 82–87 on their own.

### COMPREHENSION PROCESSES

**Remember, Understand, Apply, Analyze, Evaluate**

### PROCEDURES

**1. Reviewing Chapter 9**

**Summarizing**

Have students turn to Chapter 9 on page 72. Quickly discuss the questions from the previous Setting a Purpose. Say something like:

Yesterday, you read Chapter 9 on your own. Let's see what you found out.

What did the kids find in room 302?

(They found a man tied to a chair.)

What happened to Wallis Wallace?

(He opened his door, and two men tied him up and dragged him into Room 302.)

At the end, what did Ruth Rose say?  (She said that Mavis is really Wallis Wallace.)

**2. Introducing Chapter 10, pages 76–81**

**Defining and Using Vocabulary—suspense; Drawing Conclusions**

Say something like:

The author left us in suspense again! Do you think Ruth Rose is right?

(Yes, the man said he can't wait to go back to his cottage, but Wallis Wallace lives in a castle . . . )

Let's read to find out.

**3. First Reading**

- Ask questions and discuss the story as indicated by the blue text in this guide.
- Mix group and individual turns, independent of your voice.
  Have students work toward a group accuracy goal of 0–6 errors.
  Quietly keep track of errors made by all students in the group.
- After reading the story, practice any difficult words.
  Reread the story if students have not reached the accuracy goal.

**4. Second Reading, Short Passage Practice: Developing Prosody**

- Demonstrate expressive, fluent reading of the first paragraph. Read at a rate slightly faster than the students' rate.
- Guide practice with your voice.
- Provide individual turns while others track with their fingers and whisper read.
- Repeat with one paragraph at a time.

**Chapter 10**

"Ruth Rose, what are you talking about?" Josh said.

Dink didn't know what to think, except that he was getting a headache.

"What makes you think *I'm* Wallis Wallace?" Mavis asked.

Ruth Rose walked over to Mavis. "May I borrow your scarf?" she said.

Ruth Rose held the scarf up so everyone could see it. "When I first saw this scarf, I thought these little black letters were M's," she said. "M for Mavis."

76

She looked at Mavis Green. "But they're not M's, are they?"

She turned the scarf completely upside down. "What do they look like now?"

Dink stepped closer. "They're little W's now!"

"Right. Double-U, double-U for *Wallis Wallace!*" Ruth Rose pointed at the man. "You just said you live in a little cottage. But Wallis Wallace lives in a big *castle* in Maine. It says so on the cover of *The Silent Swamp.*"

Ruth Rose pointed at Mavis's book bag. "Seeing your bag again made me remember something I thought of today. Josh read that your castle was called Moose Manor. There's a picture of a moose on the side of your bag."

Ruth Rose handed the scarf back to Mavis. "And we read that Wallis Wallace's favorite color is green. You

**After Reading Pages 76 and 77**

**1 Understand:** Explaining
Why did Ruth Rose think Mavis Green was really Wallis Wallace?
(Her scarf had M's on it, which could also be W's. The man who was tied up said he lived in a little cottage, but Wallis Wallace lives in a castle. The castle is called Moose Manor, and Mavis has a picture of a moose on her bag . . . )

**2 Apply:** Inferring; Explaining—Solution; Using Vocabulary—mystery
Do you think she has solved the mystery? Why or why not?
(Yes, she has found Wallis Wallace. No, the man in the chair could be Wallis Wallace . . . )

78

like green ice cream, and you chose Mavis Green for your fake name."

Everyone was staring at Ruth Rose, except for the man they had untied. He started laughing.

"The cat's out of the bag now, sis," he said.

Then Mavis laughed and gave Ruth Rose a hug.

"Yes, Ruth Rose," Mavis said. "I really *am* Wallis Wallace." She put her hand on the man's shoulder. "And this is my brother, Walker Wallace. We've been planning my 'kidnapping' for weeks!"

Dink stared at Mavis, or whoever she was. "You mean Wallis Wallace is a woman?" he said.

"Yes, Dink, I'm a woman, and I'm definitely Wallis Wallace." She winked at him. "Honest!"

Mavis, the real Wallis Wallace, sat on the bed. She took off her glasses and

pulled the barrettes out of her hair. She shook her hair until it puffed out in a mass of wild curls.

"Thank goodness I can be myself now!" she said. "All day I've had to act like timid Mavis Green. I can't wait to get out of this fuddy-duddy dress and into my jeans again!"

She kicked off her shoes and wiggled her toes in the air. "Boy, does that feel good!"

Dink blinked and shook his head. Mavis Green was really Wallis Wallace? He couldn't believe it. "But why did you pretend to be kidnapped?" he asked.

The real Wallis Wallace grinned at the kids' surprised faces. "I owe you an explanation," she said.

"My new book is about a children's mystery writer who gets kidnapped. In my book, some children rescue the

## After Reading Page 78

**1 Apply:** Inferring, Explaining; Using Idioms and Expressions—cat's out of the bag
Why did the man say, "The cat's out of the bag now, sis"?
(Ruth Rose had figured out that Mavis Green was Wallis Wallace. The secret was out. The man was Wallis Wallace's brother.)

**2 Analyze:** Drawing Conclusions, **Apply:** Using Vocabulary—assume
Why did everyone think, or assume, Wallis Wallace was a man?
(They probably thought Wallis was a man's name. Her picture wasn't on any of her books, so they didn't know what she looked like . . . )

## After Reading Page 79

**1 Remember:** Identifying—What
Dink asked Mavis a very good question. What was it?
("But why did you pretend to be kidnapped?")

writer. I wanted to find out how *real* kids might solve the mystery," she explained.

She smiled at Dink. "Then your letter came, inviting me to Green Lawn. That's what gave me the idea to fake my own kidnapping. I'd become Mavis Green and watch what happened."

"Oh, yeah!" Dink said. "In your let-

ter, you said you were doing some research in Connecticut."

She nodded. "Yes, and I mentioned the word 'kidnap' in the letter to get you thinking along those lines." She smiled at the three kids. "I thought I'd have to give you more clues, but you solved the mystery all by yourselves!"

Dink laughed. "You recognized me in

**Stop Reading Here** ←

## After Reading Pages 80 and 81

**❶ Understand:** Explaining
Why did Wallis Wallace pretend to be kidnapped?
(She was doing research for her new book. She wanted to find out how real kids would solve a mystery . . . )

**❷ Evaluate:** Responding
How would you feel if you were Dink or Ruth Rose?
(I would be proud that I figured out the case. I would be mad that Wallis Wallace tricked us. I would be happy that Wallis Wallace wasn't kidnapped after all . . . )

## CHAPTER 10 INSTRUCTIONS

Students read Chapter 10, pages 82–87, without the teacher, independently or with partners.

## COMPREHENSION PROCESSES

**Understand, Apply**

## PROCEDURES FOR READING ON YOUR OWN

1. **Getting Ready**

   Have students turn to page 81. Tell them they will begin reading at the last line at the bottom of the page.

2. **Setting a Purpose**

   **Explaining; Inferring; Using Vocabulary—recognize, dedicate**

   Before students begin reading, say something like:

   As you read the next pages, try to answer:
   - Why doesn't Wallis Wallace want people to recognize her?
   - Why is Wallis Wallace going to dedicate her next book to Dink, Josh, and Ruth Rose?

3. **Reading on Your Own: Partner or Whisper Reading**
   - Have students take turns reading every other page with a partner or have students whisper read pages 82–87 on their own.
   - Continue having students track each word with their fingers.

4. **Comprehension and Skill Work**

   Tell students they will do Case Log Entry 8 and Comprehension and Skill Activities 8a and 8b after they read on their own. Guide practice, as needed. For teacher directions, see pages 132–135.

5. **Homework 8: New Passage**

**PREP NOTE**

**Setting a Purpose**

Write questions on a chalkboard, white board, or large piece of paper before working with your small group.

82

the bookstore from my picture," he said. "And you didn't send *me* a picture so I wouldn't recognize *you!*"

"Then my nutty sister dragged *me* into her plan," Walker Wallace said. "I should be home checking my lobster pots."

"While you were eating lunch, Walker and I ate ours up here," Wallis said. "Then, just before two o'clock, I tied him in the chair and ran downstairs to meet you out front as Mavis."

Wallis Wallace threw back her head and laughed. "Do you remember downstairs when Dink said there was something fishy on the third floor?"

She got up and stood next to her brother. "Well, I'm always teasing Walker about smelling fishy from handling his lobster bait. So when you said something was *fishy* in the hotel, I had to pretend to cough so you wouldn't

know I was really laughing!"

"Boy, did you have us fooled," Dink said.

Wallis Wallace grinned. "Mr. Paskey was in on it. I had to tell him the truth. As you saw this morning at the Book Nook, my little scheme made him very nervous. I've promised him I'll come back and do a real book signing soon. But I'll be in disguise, so be prepared for anything!"

Dink shook his head. "I was so disappointed because I couldn't meet my favorite author this morning," he said. "And I've been with you all day and didn't even know it!"

She looked at Dink. "I'm so sorry I tricked you. Will you forgive me?"

Dink blushed. "Sure."

"I have a question," Josh said. "Where did you really sleep last night?"

"Right here in Room 302. A few

*84*

weeks ago, I telephoned to reserve two rooms next to each other. Last night, I checked into Room 303 as Wallis Wallace, the man. Up in Room 303, I took off the hat and coat and sunglasses. Then I sneaked back down to the lobby wearing a blond wig. I checked in again, this time into Room 302."

"Did you smudge the signature?" Ruth Rose asked.

"Oh, you noticed that!" Wallis said. "I'm so used to signing my real name in books, I started to write *Wallis*. So I 'accidentally' smudged it."

"I have a question, Mavis, I mean Miss Wallace...what should we call you?" Dink asked.

"My friends call me Wallis," she said.

"Well, the taxi driver told us you were smiling in the taxi. What were you smiling about?"

Wallis Wallace was smiling now.

"Oh, about a lot of things. First, I was wearing a man's disguise, and that made me feel pretty silly. And I knew I was going to meet you, one of my biggest fans. And I was happy because I knew whatever happened, the next day would be fun!"

"I sure had fun," Josh said, grinning. "Poor Mr. Paskey, having to lie to everyone with a straight face!"

"Boy, did I have a hard time pretending to be Mavis all day," Wallis said. "But my plan worked. I met three brilliant detectives. You helped me to see how real kids would investigate a kidnapping. Now I can go back to Maine and finish my book."

"How come your book jackets never say that you're a woman?" Ruth Rose asked.

Wallis Wallace smiled. "Because of my name, most people assume that I'm

86

a man," she explained. "I let them think that so I can do my research easier. I've learned that people clam up if they know I'm Wallis Wallace. So out in public I pretend I'm Mavis Green, just a regular person, not a mystery writer."

"I get it!" Dink said. "You don't have your picture on your books so people can't recognize you."

"Right. And I hope you'll keep my secret."

"We will. Right, guys?" Ruth Rose said.

"Thank you! Any more questions?" Wallis asked.

"Yeah," Walker said, giving his sister a look. "When do we leave? I've got lobsters waiting for me."

"I have a question, too," Dink said. "Will you send me your picture now?"

"Yes, but I'll do better than that," Wallis said. "I'll dedicate my next book to my three new friends!"

Dink, Josh, and Ruth Rose did a triple high five.

"Excuse me," Mr. Linkletter said from the door where he had been standing.

They all looked at him.

"It's nearly checkout time."

Everyone laughed.

Mr. Linkletter smiled, but just a little.

### ENTRY 8

### COMPREHENSION PROCESSES

**Understand**

### WRITING TRAITS

**Conventions—Capital**

### PROCEDURES

Discuss each step. Then have students complete the page independently.

**Note Taking: Summarizing—Basic Instructions**

Have students read the case notes and fill in the blanks. Remind students to use capitals for proper names.

Identifying—What, Who; Sentence Completion Using Vocabulary— disguise, impressed, perfect

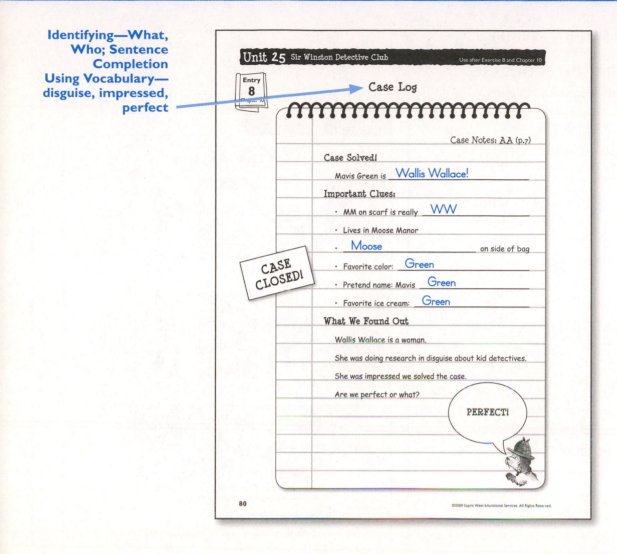

**Unit 25** Sir Winston Detective Club      Use after Exercise 8 and Chapter 10

Entry **8** (Chapter 10)

## Case Log

Case Notes: AA (p.7)

Case Solved!

Mavis Green is _Wallis Wallace!_

Important Clues:

· MM on scarf is really _WW_

· Lives in Moose Manor

· _Moose_ on side of bag

· Favorite color: _Green_

· Pretend name: Mavis _Green_

· Favorite ice cream: _Green_

What We Found Out

Wallis Wallace is a woman.

She was doing research in disguise about kid detectives.

She was impressed we solved the case.

Are we perfect or what?

PERFECT!

CASE CLOSED!

80

## BEST MAIN CHARACTER(S)

### COMPREHENSION PROCESSES

Understand, Evaluate, Create

### WRITING TRAITS

Conventions—Capital

Viewing, Responding

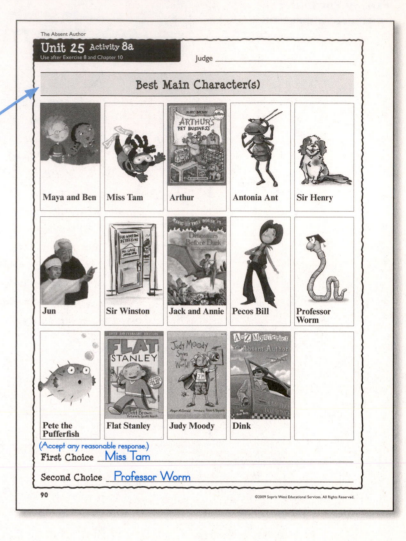

### PROCEDURES

For each step, demonstrate and guide practice, as needed. Then have students complete the page independently.

**Personal Response—Specific Instructions**

• Have students write a first and second choice for their favorite storybook characters at the bottom of Activity 8a.

• For Activity 8b, have students fill in the blank for their favorite trade book and check a box with their choices for favorite *Read Well* book and main character.

## FINAL SECRET BALLOT

**Viewing, Responding** ⟶

The Absent Author

**Unit 25** Activity **8b**
Use after Exercise 8 and Chapter 10

Judge _____

### Final Secret Ballot
(Accept any reasonable response.)

| Category | Ballot |
|---|---|
| **Best Trade Book** (See page 85, Activity 6b) | My choice for best trade book is: <br> _Dinosaurs Before Dark_ |
| **Best _Read Well_ Book** | My choice for best _Read Well_ storybook is: <br> ☐ Our World, Our Home <br> ☐ Communities <br> ☐ From Generation to Generation <br> ☐ All About Dinosaurs <br> ☐ Spiders and Bats <br> ☐ Young America <br> ☐ Science Digest: Food Chains <br> ☑ The Reef <br> ☐ A Great Man <br> ☐ Science Digest: Where in the World? |
| **Best Main Character** | My choice for best main character is: <br> ☐ Maya and Ben ☐ Jack and Annie <br> ☑ Miss Tam ☐ Pecos Bill <br> ☐ Arthur ☐ Professor Worm <br> ☐ Antonia Ant ☐ Pete the Pufferfish <br> ☐ Sir Henry ☐ Flat Stanley <br> ☐ Jun ☐ Judy Moody <br> ☐ Sir Winston ☐ Dink |

91

## PASSAGE INSTRUCTIONS

This Story Reading targets fluency as the primary goal of instruction and practice.

Students do repeated readings of this passage to improve accuracy and expression.

*Note:* This passage is found in *Exercise Book 4*, Unit 25, Closing Ceremonies, or pages 75–77.

## COMPREHENSION PROCESSES

**Understand, Apply, Analyze, Evaluate**

## PROCEDURES

1. **Warm-Up: Partner Reading or Whisper Reading**

   Before beginning group Story Reading, have students finger track and partner or whisper read the selection.

2. **First Reading**

   • Mix group and individual turns, independent of your voice.
   Have students work toward a group accuracy goal of 0–2 errors.
   Quietly keep track of errors made by all students in the group.

   • After reading the story, practice any difficult words.
   Reread the story if students have not reached the accuracy goal.

3. **Optional Second Reading, Short Passage Practice: Developing Prosody**

   When students reach "Best *Read Well* Book of the Year, Presented by a T. Rex Named Sue," you may wish to have them read their opinions about their favorite *Read Well* storybook from Comp & Skill Activity 7b.

4. **Homework 9: Repeated Reading**

The Absent Author

## Unit 25 Closing Ceremonies (1 of 3)

### The Annual *Read Well* Literary Awards

*by Marilyn Sprick and Ann Watanabe*
*illustrated by Page Eastburn O'Rourke,*
*Janet Pederson, Jana Christy,*
*and Steve Clark*

Lights, camera, action!

#### Live From the Red Carpet With Itsy Bitsy

Good evening.  It's Itsy Bitsy Spider here, live at the Annual *Read Well* Literary Awards.  It's the day that many of the nominees have awaited.  World traveler Miss Tam arrived early and has already taken a leisurely stroll down the red carpet.  As is her habit, Miss Tam was calm and her usual cheerful self.  She was wearing her shiny red dress shoes and her special retirement dress.  Minnie Bird and Scraggly Cat were with Miss Tam.

There's a bit of an uproar from the crowd.  On the red carpet now is that popular pair—Sir Henry and Sir Winston.  Sir Henry has on his famous goggles and scarf.  Look, Sir Winston has his nose to the ground.  Let's see if we can get a word with him.  Sir Winston, Sir Winston! Can we have a moment with you? Can you tell us what you are sniffing?

Sorry folks, Sir Winston seems to have picked up a scent.  He has left the red carpet and is following his nose.

It looks like it's time to turn the show over to Slue-Foot Sue.  She is inside the Awards Hall where our celebrities are waiting for the presentations to begin.

75

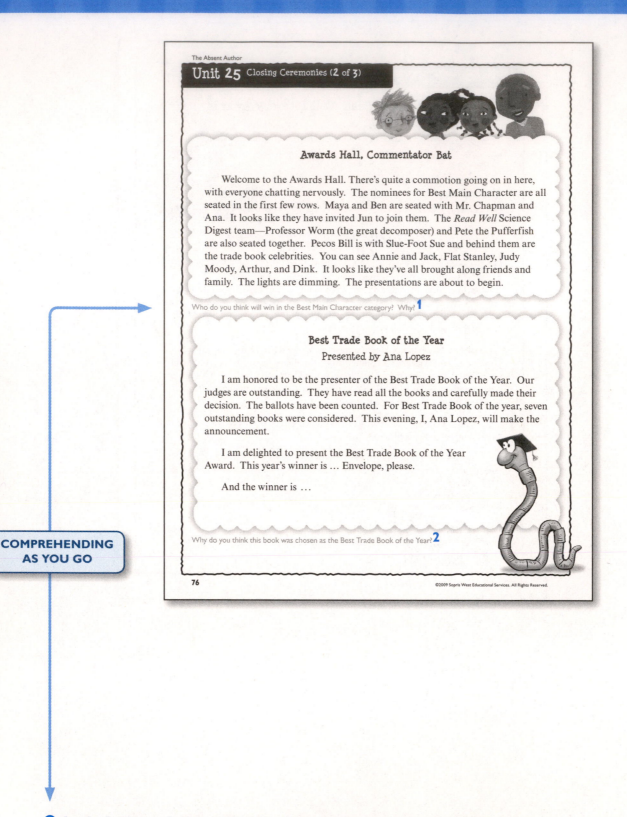

The Absent Author

## Unit 25  Closing Ceremonies (2 of 3)

### Awards Hall, Commentator Bat

Welcome to the Awards Hall. There's quite a commotion going on in here, with everyone chatting nervously. The nominees for Best Main Character are all seated in the first few rows. Maya and Ben are seated with Mr. Chapman and Ana. It looks like they have invited Jun to join them. The *Read Well* Science Digest team—Professor Worm (the great decomposer) and Pete the Pufferfish are also seated together. Pecos Bill is with Slue-Foot Sue and behind them are the trade book celebrities. You can see Annie and Jack, Flat Stanley, Judy Moody, Arthur, and Dink. It looks like they've all brought along friends and family. The lights are dimming. The presentations are about to begin.

Who do you think will win in the Best Main Character category? Why? **1**

### Best Trade Book of the Year
#### Presented by Ana Lopez

I am honored to be the presenter of the Best Trade Book of the Year. Our judges are outstanding. They have read all the books and carefully made their decision. The ballots have been counted. For Best Trade Book of the year, seven outstanding books were considered. This evening, I, Ana Lopez, will make the announcement.

I am delighted to present the Best Trade Book of the Year Award. This year's winner is … Envelope, please.

And the winner is …

Why do you think this book was chosen as the Best Trade Book of the Year? **2**

**COMPREHENDING AS YOU GO**

76

©2009 Sopris West Educational Services. All Rights Reserved.

**❶ Apply:** Predicting; Explaining; Using Vocabulary—adventure (Miss Tam will win because she has such interesting adventures. Flat Stanley will win because his book was the funniest . . . )

**❷ Analyze:** Drawing Conclusions (I think *Dinosaurs Before Dark* won because kids like to read about dinosaurs. I think *Flat Stanley* won because it was the funniest book we read . . . )

The Absent Author

## Unit 25  Closing Ceremonies (3 of 3)

### Best *Read Well* Book of the Year
Presented by a T. Rex Named Sue

How do you do?  I am Sue.  I am happy to present the Best *Read Well* Book of the Year.  For this category, our judges have written opinions of their choices.

Reading the opinions are …

Envelope, please. And the winner is …

Why do you think this book was chosen as the *Read Well* Book of the Year?[1]  Do you agree or disagree and why?[2]

### Best Main Character of the Year
Presented by Thor and Emily

Emily and I are pleased to be here to help present the most important award of the evening—Best Main Character in a piece of fiction.

Our judges had many choices—each character has exceptional qualities as created by a dedicated group of children's writers.

Envelope, please. And the winner is …

As is the custom, there is quite a commotion in the hall now.  Everyone is hugging and shaking hands.  It's been an eventful year.

### Congratulations to all and to all a good night!

Who is being congratulated?[3]  The *Read Well* authors are also congratulating you!  Do you know why?[4]

77

**COMPREHENDING AS YOU GO**

❶ **Analyze:** Drawing Conclusions; **Apply:** Using Vocabulary—fascinating  (I think [*Science Digest: Food Chains*] won because [it was fascinating to read about lions and other animals.  There were lots of interesting articles in the *Science Digest* . . . ])

❷ **Evaluate:** Making Judgments  (I agree with the choice because I learned a lot from reading [the *Science Digest*].  I disagree because I enjoyed reading [*All About Dinosaurs*] more.  I like fiction better than nonfiction . . . )

❸ **Apply:** Inferring, Explaining  (Everyone is being congratulated.)

❹ **Apply:** Inferring, Explaining; **Understand:** Using Vocabulary—congratulate, amazing  (They are congratulating us because we are at the end of the program.  They are congratulating us because we are amazing readers . . . )

## JUST FOR FUN • *READ WELL* LITERARY AWARD

The Absent Author

**Unit 25**
Use anytime

Name _____

### Just for Fun • *Read Well* Literary Award

Draw a picture of your favorite main character on the trophy. Then complete the sentence that tells who your main character is, and explain why that's your favorite character.
(Accept any reasonable response.)

Read Well Literary Award

The Best Main Character

My choice for the best main character is __Miss Tam.__
__She was so much fun to read about!  I liked__
__her adventures around the world.  I liked__
__her same old habits.  Scraggly Cat__
__and Minnie Bird were great__
__pets.  They were pretty__
__funny too!__

92                                              ©2009 Sopris West Educational Services. All Rights Reserved.

---

**HOW TO USE "JUST FOR FUN" ACTIVITIES**

*Note:* This activity is optional and is *just for fun.* Use the activity:
• as a cushion activity
• for homework
• just for fun

---

### PROCEDURES

As time allows, have students draw a picture of their choice for Best Main Character in the box. Have them write the name of the character on the line below their illustration. Then have them write reasons for their choice in the lines provided.

This page may be given to students as homework.

# End of the Unit

## In this section, you will find:

### Oral Reading Fluency Assessment

As you near the end of the unit, plan to give the Oral Reading Fluency Assessment to each child in your group. Unit 25 Oral Reading Fluency Assessment is located on page 143 and in the *Assessment Manual*.

*Note:* Using the Flesch-Kincaid Grade Level readability formula, the Unit 25 Assessment has a 3.5 readability level.

According to Hasbrouck and Tindal (2006), students at the end of second grade read at approximately the following percentile ranks based on words correct per minute. Students who have been held to mastery are reading anywhere from the 75th to the 99th percentile.

| WCPM | PERCENTILE RANK |
|------|-----------------|
| 142  | 90              |
| 117  | 75              |
| 89   | 50              |

### Celebrations!

The focus of the end of this unit is on celebration and accomplishments. No written assessment is included.

# Acknowledging Accomplishments

## PROCEDURES

Before copying the certificate and parent letter on page 144, determine how you wish to complete the letter. A few options are listed below.

### OPTION 1: A GROUP ACCOMPLISHMENT, TEACHER GENERATED

You may wish to conserve instructional time by filling out the parent letter on page 144 before copying it.

1. Write a group accomplishment such as "I am especially proud that I completed *Read Well 2 Plus!*" or "I am especially proud that I can read sophisticated biographies, nonfiction, and literature" on the blackline master.

2. Copy the blackline master.

3. Fill in the individual student information at the top of the certificate.
   • Write in the Unit 25 words correct per minute score.
   • Write in the number of words gained since the beginning of the year.

4. Have students co-sign the letter before taking it home.

### OPTION 2: INDIVIDUAL ACCOMPLISHMENT, TEACHER GENERATED

1. Copy the blackline master.

2. Fill in the individual student information at the top of the certificate.
   • Write in the Unit 25 words correct per minute.
   • Write in the number of words gained since the beginning of the year.

3. Meet with each child and tailor his or her accomplishment. For example, compare the individual's fluency at the beginning of *Read Well 2* with his or her average fluency across the last three units.

4. Have students co-sign the letter before taking it home.

### OPTION 3: INDIVIDUAL ACCOMPLISHMENT, STUDENT GENERATED

1. Copy the blackline master.

2. Fill in the individual student information at the top of the certificate.
   • Write in the Unit 25 words correct per minute.
   • Write in the number of words gained since the beginning of the year.

3. During group time, have students fill out their own form. Quickly brainstorm with students about possible accomplishments. Suggestions include: "I am especially proud of . . . "
   • completing Comprehension and Skill Work neatly and on time.
   • using expression when reading.
   • taking home and returning my homework on time.
   • reading well with a partner.
   • reading with 100% accuracy on my last assessment.

4. Have students co-sign the letter before taking it home.

## TRICKY WORD and FOCUS SKILL WARM-UP

| lose | glistening | peculiar | laughed | mischievous |
|------|-----------|----------|---------|-------------|

## ORAL READING FLUENCY PASSAGE

### A Mystery

★"How peculiar. My watch has disappeared," said     7

Emma's mother. "I put it right here on the picnic table, and now     20

it's gone." Emma helped her search for the watch. They couldn't     31

locate it anywhere.     34

     The next day, Emma put her shiny ring on the porch so     46

she wouldn't lose it while she was playing. When she came back,     58

it had disappeared. Emma and her mother rummaged around the     68

yard again.     70

     Then Emma saw something glistening in the sun over by     80

the enormous oak tree. She quickly ran to the tree and discovered     92

the watch and the ring on the ground beneath it. But how did     106

they get way over by the big oak tree?     114

     She looked up. A mischievous crow sat on a branch with     125

a shiny silver button in its beak! The bird winked at Emma,     137

gave a muffled squawk, and dropped the button. Emma's mother     147

laughed and said, "Oh my! I have heard that crows like to collect     160

shiny things. Mystery solved!"     164

| | |
|---|---|
| **ORAL READING FLUENCY** | Start timing at the ★. Mark errors. Make a single slash in the text (/) at 60 seconds. Have the student complete the passage. If the student completes the passage in less than 60 seconds, have the student go back to the ★ and continue reading. Make a double slash in the text (//) at 60 seconds. |
| **WCPM** | Determine words correct per minute by subtracting errors from words read in 60 seconds. |
| **STRONG PASS** | The student scores no more than 2 errors on the first pass through the passage and reads 133 or more words correct per minute. |
| **PASS** | The student scores no more than 2 errors on the first pass through the passage and reads 112 to 132 words correct per minute. |
| | Assess for placement in a 3² (mid–third grade) or 4¹ (early fourth grade) reading program. |

# Congratulations!

On this _____ day of _____, _____,
you have successfully completed

## Read Well 2 Plus

Unit 25 Assessment: _____ WCPM. You improved your score by _____ WCPM since Unit _____!

Dear _____,

I read many fascinating books during Read Well 2. My favorite trade book was _____

My favorite Read Well storybook was _____

My favorite character was _____

I am especially proud of _____

Sincerely,

_____

and _____